A NEW COMPANION TO SHAKESPEARE STUDIES

EDITED BY
KENNETH MUIR
AND
S. SCHOENBAUM

CAMBRIDGE UNIVERSITY PRESS

CAMBRIDGE
LONDON · NEW YORK · MELBOURNE

Published by the Syndics of the Cambridge University Press
The Pitt Building, Trumpington Street, Cambridge CB2 IRP
Bentley House, 200 Euston Road, London NW1 2DB
32 East 57th Street, New York, NY 10022, USA
296 Beaconsfield Parade, Middle Park, Melbourne 3206, Australia

Library of Congress catalogue card number: 78-118066

ISBN: 0 521 07941 1 hard covers
ISBN: 0 521 09645 6 paperback

First published 1971
Reprinted 1972 1974 1976 1979

Printed in Great Britain at the
University Press, Cambridge

CONTENTS

ILLUSTRATIONS

PREFACE

The first *Companion to Shakespeare Studies*, edited by Harley Granville-Barker and G. B. Harrison, was published in 1934. It has been in constant demand ever since; and the present volume attempts, with some difference of emphasis, to fulfil a similar need. Shakespeare criticism has so proliferated during the last thirty-five years that both the student and the general reader need a guide to the most important developments. We had to select from a much larger series of topics, and some of those we had to omit are discussed in *Shakespeare Survey 17* ('Shakespeare in his Own Age'). All the contributors to the former companion were British, with the possible exception of T. S. Eliot. We have obtained contributions from both sides of the Atlantic.

K.M.
S.S.

1

THE LIFE OF SHAKESPEARE

S. SCHOENBAUM

'All that is known with any degree of certainty concerning Shake-speare, is – that he was born at Stratford upon Avon, – married and had children there, – went to London, where he commenced actor, and wrote poems and plays, returned to Stratford, made his will, died, and was buried.' Thus wrote a great Shakespearian scholar of the eighteenth century, George Steevens. His remark has been often quoted, and others have made essentially the same comment in less memorable words. But Steevens exaggerated, and since his time much has been learned about the poet, his ancestors and family, and his Stratford and London associations. These facts, it is true, are of a public character, and are recorded in official, mainly legal, documents – con-veyances of property, tax assessments and the like; as such, they afford no insight into the interior life of the artist, wherein resides the chief fascination of literary biography. Yet we know more about Shake-speare than about most of his fellow playwrights. John Webster, for example, the author of two great tragedies, remains little more than an elusive ghost. And, however impersonal, what we know about Shakespeare is not without interest or meaning.

The parish register of Holy Trinity Church records his baptism on 26 April 1564. Tradition assigns his birthdate to the twenty-third. An interval of three days between birth and christening is not unlikely, and supporting evidence is provided by the inscription on the drama-tist's tomb, which states that he died on 23 April 1616, in his fifty-third year. But the date of Shakespeare's birth is not precisely known, and behind the conventional assignment lurks the urge to have the National Poet born on the day of St George, patron saint of England; the wish is father of many a tradition. The register of Stratford Church records also the baptism of seven brothers and sisters. Of these, three – Margaret, Anne, and the first Joan (another Joan was christened later) – died in childhood. The infant William may himself have narrowly escaped mortality, for the plague gripped Stratford in 1564, carrying off over 200 souls in six months. Of the surviving siblings, most interest attaches to the playwright's youngest brother Edmund, christened on 3 May 1580; he became an actor in London, where he died young. He was buried in December 1607 in St Saviour's Church in Southwark.

The name of Shakespeare is of great antiquity in Warwickshire: as far back as 1248 a William Sakspere of Clopton was hanged for robbery. John Shakespeare, the dramatist's father, was probably the eldest son of Richard, a husbandman of Snitterfield, a village some three miles north of Stratford. This Richard Shakespeare held lands as a tenant on a manor belonging to Robert Arden, a gentleman of worship in the hamlet of Wilmcote, north-west of Stratford. Arden's youngest daughter Mary inherited from him the Asbies estate of fifty acres when he died in 1556. Shortly thereafter she married John Shakespeare.

He had by 1552 migrated to Stratford, and there set himself up as a glover and whittawer (curer and whitener of skins), an occupation requiring a seven-year apprenticeship. He prospered. In addition to his glove business, he is known to have sold barley, timber, and wool. In 1556 he bought a house, with garden and croft, in Greenhill Street, and a house adjoining the one he already occupied in Henley Street. Tradition identifies the double house in Henley Street as the poet's birthplace. Civic recognition came to John Shakespeare: first appointed to minor offices – inspector of ale and bread, constable, affeeror (assessor of fines not determined by the statutes) – he became, in turn, chamberlain, member of the town council, one of the fourteen aldermen privileged to wear a black cloth gown trimmed with fur, and finally, in 1568, high bailiff (the equivalent today of mayor). Yet he was probably illiterate, for no signature exists for him. He signed documents with his mark, a pair of glover's compasses, or with a cross.

Some time in the mid-seventies John Shakespeare considered applying for a grant of arms, but nothing came of it, apparently because he had fallen on hard times. After 1575 he purchased no more property. The aldermen excused him, in 1578, from paying his 4d. weekly tax for poor relief. He stopped attending council meetings, and in 1586 was deprived of his alderman's gown. He contracted debts, and had to mortgage part of his wife's inheritance. In 1592 he appears in a list of persons 'heretofore presented for not coming monthly to the church according to Her Majesty's laws'; the document has been interpreted as offering evidence of John Shakespeare's recusancy, but a note appended to it indicates that he avoided services 'for fear of process for debt', arrests by sheriff's officers being then permitted on Sunday. (That he subscribed to the old faith is, however, possible, and is supported by a Spiritual Last Will and Testament, a Catholic profession attributed to 'John Shakspear' and purportedly found in the roof of the Henley Street homestead in the eighteenth century; however, this document, since lost, is of doubtful authenticity.) John's straitened circumstances forced him, before 1590, to part with his house on Greenhill Street, but he never became so desperate that he had to sell his Henley Street dwelling. The grant of arms that in 1596 conferred the status of gentleman on John Shakespeare was probably instigated by his son, who had by then succeeded handsomely in the London theatrical world.

Fortunately the education of his children cost him nothing. According to Nicholas Rowe, who published the first connected life of Shakespeare in 1709, the dramatist's father bred him 'for some time at a free school'. Although records for pupils at the King's New School of Stratford-upon-Avon in the sixteenth century have not come down, there is no reason to doubt Rowe. It was a superior institution of its kind: the masters during Shakespeare's boyhood held bachelor's and master's degrees from Oxford University, and received good remuneration – £20 a year plus a dwelling – by the standards of the day. A child entering at about the age of five probably passed his first two or three years at an attached petty school where, under the tuition of the usher, he mastered the alphabet and learned the rudiments of reading and writing. Then, at the grammar school proper, he spent long hours – from seven until eleven in the morning, and one to five in the afternoon – memorizing by rote his Latin grammar, an experience perhaps ruefully recalled in *The Merry Wives of Windsor* when the Welsh pedagogue Sir Hugh Evans puts little William through a model interrogation for the benefit of his disgruntled mother:

EVANS   Show me now, William, some declensions of your pronouns.
WILLIAM   Forsooth, I have forgot.
EVANS   It is *qui, quae, quod*; if you forget your *qui's*, your *quae's*, and your *quod's*, you must be preeches [i.e., flogged].

Having survived Lily's *Grammatica Latina*, the scholars moved on to their Latin axioms and phrases, then to *Aesop's Fables* and the *Eclogues* of Baptista Spagnuoli Mantuanus ('Old Mantuan, old Mantuan!' ecstatically declares Holofernes the schoolmaster in *Love's Labour's Lost*, 'Who understandeth thee not, loves thee not'). There followed literary classics – Vergil, perhaps Horace, Plautus or Terence (sometimes acted by the children), and especially Ovid, who would remain the dramatist's favourite – as well as training in rhetoric (Cicero) and history: Caesar or Sallust. Thus Shakespeare acquired the small Latin with which Jonson credits him; possibly in the upper forms he obtained his 'less Greek'. How long Shakespeare attended the free school we can only guess. Rowe, whose information derives from Stratford traditions, reports that the father was forced, because of 'the narrow-ness of his circumstances, and the want of his assistance at home...to withdraw him from thence'.

For the next episode in Shakespeare's life better documentation is available. On 28 November 1582 the Bishop of Worcester, in whose diocese Stratford lay, issued a bond authorizing the marriage of 'William Shagspere' and 'Anne Hathwey of Stratford' after one asking of the banns, rather than the customary three. (Pronouncement of the banns in church allowed members of the congregation to come forward if they knew of any hindrance to the match.) Fulke Sandells and John Richardson, the friends of the bride's family who signed the bond, obligated themselves to pay the Bishop or his officials £40 should any action be brought against them for issuance of the licence. The licence itself is not preserved, nor is any record of the ceremony.[1] Of Anne Hathaway we know little, except that she was probably the eldest daughter of Richard, a husbandman living at Hewlands Farm in Shottery, a hamlet a mile west of Stratford; on this property stands the thatched farmhouse today known as Anne Hathaway's Cottage. In his will, dated 1 September 1581 and drawn up shortly before his death, Hathaway mentions no daughter Anne, but the names Anne and Agnes were used interchangeably, and the latter is bequeathed ten marks (£6 13s. 4d.) to be paid to her on her wedding day. At the time of the marriage she was twenty-six, and the groom eighteen. An entry in the Stratford register recording the baptism on 26 May 1583 of Susanna daughter to William Shakespeare may help to explain why he married so early. On 2 February 1585 his twins, Hamnet and Judith, were christened at Holy Trinity. They were named after lifelong family friends, Hamnet and Judith Sadler; years later Hamnet, a baker of Stratford, witnessed the poet's will and was remembered in it.

Between the birth of the twins in 1585 and the first reference to Shakespeare in London in 1592 no records exist, and the so-called Lost Years have occasioned much speculation. The seventeenth-century gossip Aubrey reported, on the authority of the actor William Beeston (whose father knew Shakespeare) that 'he had been in his younger years a schoolmaster in the country' – a suggestion that has met with unsurprising favour on the part of academic biographers. The circumstances of the poet's departure from Stratford are the sub-ject of a celebrated legend which Rowe included in his Life:

He had, by a misfortune common enough to young fellows, fallen into ill company; and, amongst them, some that made a frequent practice of deer-stealing engaged him with them more than once in robbing a park that belonged to Sir Thomas Lucy of Cherlecot, near Stratford. For this he was prosecuted by that gentleman, as he thought, somewhat too severely; and in order to revenge that ill usage, he made a ballad upon him. And though this, probably the first essay of his poetry, be lost, yet it is said to have been so very bitter, that it redoubled the prosecution against him to that degree that he was obliged to leave his business and family in Warwickshire for some time, and shelter himself in London.

A somewhat earlier version of the same story recorded by Richard Davies, rector of Sapperton, has Shakespeare 'much given to all unluckiness in stealing venison and rabbits, particularly from Sir —— Lucy, who had him oft whipped and sometimes imprisoned and at last made him fly his native country, to his great advancement'. For centuries accepted unhesitantly by most biographers, the deer-poaching tradition has certain inherent improbabilities (Lucy, for example, did not then have a park at Charlecote) and is now consigned to the Shakespeare mythos, although a few responsible scholars – notably Sir Edmund Chambers and G. E. Bentley – are willing to allow it a possible grain of truth.

Shakespeare may have joined one of the touring companies – Leicester's, Warwick's, the Queen's – that played at Stratford in the eighties; the Queen's men, we know, lacked a player in the summer of 1587. By 1592 Shakespeare had established himself in the London theatrical world as actor and playwright, for in that year he was subjected to a venomous attack by another dramatist, Robert Greene. In his *Groatsworth of Wit, Bought with a Million of Repentance*, written as he lay dying, Greene warns his friends – fellow playwrights trained up (unlike Shakespeare) in the university – against 'those puppets. . . that spake from our mouths, those antics garnished in our colours', and particularly against one:

an upstart crow, beautified with our feathers, that with his *Tiger's heart wrapped in a player's hide*, supposes he is as well able to bombast out a blank verse as the best of you: and being an absolute *Johannes fac totum*, is in his own conceit the only Shake-scene in a country.

The punning reference to a Shake-scene and the parody of a line from *3 Henry VI* ('O tiger's heart wrapp'd in a woman's hide!') identify the victim unmistakably. Less clear is the purport of the attack, couched as it is in obscurely allusive language; but Greene seems to be sneering at a mere player, one of the 'antics garnished in our colours', who deigns to set himself up as a universal genius (*Johannes fac totum*) and to rival his betters by turning out plays in stilted blank verse. The notice, however hostile, pays tribute to a successful competitor.

The *Groatsworth of Wit* stirred protest which, Greene being dead, fell on the head of the man who had prepared the manuscript for the printers. Before the year was out Henry Chettle had included, in the prefatory address to his *Kind Heart's Dream*, a handsome apology to the actor-playwright: 'I am as sorry as if the original fault had been my fault, because myself have seen his demeanour no less civil than he excellent in the quality [i.e. acting] he professes. Besides, divers of worship have reported his uprightness of dealing, which argues his honesty, and his facetious grace in writing, that approves his art.'

Who the divers of worship were that vouched for Shakespeare's good character is not recorded. We do know, however, that in the next year, 1593, he published *Venus and Adonis* with a dedication to Henry Wriothesley, third Earl of Southampton and Baron Titchfield. The respectfully formal terms with which the patron, then nineteen, is addressed do not argue close personal acquaintance on the poet's part, but a warmer note enters into the dedication, the next year, of *The Rape of Lucrece* to the same nobleman:

The love I dedicate to your Lordship is without end; whereof this pamphlet, without beginning, is but a superfluous moiety. The warrant I have of your honourable disposition, not the worth of my untutored lines, makes it assured of acceptance. What I have done is yours; what I have to do is yours; being part in all I have, devoted yours.

Both poems issued from the press of a former Stratford neighbour, Richard Field, whose father's goods John Shakespeare had appraised in 1592; Field, three years William's senior, had migrated to London in 1579. What dealings, if any, Shakespeare had with Southampton after the appearance of the two poems can only be conjectured, and of speculation there has been a sufficiency. No further document links the two men; the Earl is not one of the patrons to whom Shakespeare's old friends and colleagues, Heminges and Condell, dedicated the First Folio of his works in 1623. Many believe that Southampton is the Fair Youth celebrated in the Sonnets, and although this is possible, it cannot, in the nature of things, be demonstrated.

Shakespeare wrote *Venus and Adonis* and *The Rape of Lucrece* during the catastrophic plague season that halted London theatrical activity from the summer of 1592 until the spring of 1594. Non-dramatic writing cannot have diverted Shakespeare more than temporarily from his principal occupation. During the Christmas festivities of 1594 the Lord Chamberlain's men acted two plays before Queen Elizabeth at court, and the following March, Shakespeare along with William Kempe and Richard Burbage signed a receipt for the company's honorarium of £20. Kempe was then the outstanding comedian of the age; Burbage would soon gain equal pre-eminence as a tragedian. This first extant reference to Shakespeare as a member of a troupe thus shows him already fully established and representing his company in an official capacity. Burbage is again associated with the dramatist in a scurrilous anecdote that John Manningham, a young law student, jotted down in his commonplace book in 1602:

Upon a time when Burbage played Richard the Third there was a citizen grew so far in liking with him that before she went from the play she appointed him to come that night unto her by the name of Richard the Third. Shakespeare, overhearing their conclusion, went before, was entertained and at his game ere Burbage came. Then message being brought that Richard the Third was at the door, Shakespeare caused return to be made that William the Conqueror was before Richard the Third.

The story may or may not be true.

About another aspect of Shakespeare's career we have surer information: he acted in 1598 in Jonson's *Every Man in His Humour* and, in 1603, in the same author's *Sejanus*. From traditions of uncertain reliability we learn that Shakespeare played 'kingly parts', and that he took the roles of the faithful old servant Adam in *As You Like It* and the Ghost in *Hamlet*. He was not one of the celebrated actors of the period, although Aubrey reports that he 'did act exceedingly well'.

When in 1598 the Lord Chamberlain's men tore down their regular playhouse, the Theatre, and used the timber to build the Globe, they set up a species of proprietorship in which (as a later document shows) Shakespeare was entitled to 10 per cent of the profits. These were considerable, although over the years the value of Shakespeare's share fluctuated, depending upon the number of shareholders. As part-owner he of course helped to direct company policy. Thus he served his troupe in a triple capacity: as playwright, actor, and business director.

In the royal patent by which the Lord Chamberlain's men became, in 1603, the King's men, Shakespeare's name appears near the head of the list. The next year he is the first mentioned of the nine players allowed cloth for new liveries in order to participate, as grooms of the King's chamber, in the coronation procession.

Shakespeare lived near where he worked. From tax assessments we know that before October 1596 he dwelt in St Helen's, Bishopsgate, a short distance from the Theatre, and that later (by October 1599) he had moved across the river to the Liberty of the Clink on the Bankside, where, in Southwark, the Globe stood. He may have been living on the Bankside as early as Michaelmas Term, 1596, when one William Wayte swore the peace against William Shakspere, Francis Langley, and two unknown women. This Langley owned the new Swan playhouse; Wayte was the stepson and instrument of William Gardiner, a litigious Surrey Justice of the Peace who sought to put the theatre out of business. The nature of Shakespeare's involvement in this feud remains a mystery; possibly he was a mere bystander.

Some time before 1604 he was lodging – for how long is not certain – with the family of a French Huguenot tiremaker (i.e. manufacturer of ladies' ornamental headdresses) in Silver Street, near St Olave's church in north-west London. So much we learn from a suit brought against Mountjoy in 1612 by his son-in-law and former apprentice, Stephen Belott. The documents in the action afford a rare personal glimpse of Shakespeare. The Mountjoys were eager to marry their daughter Mary, an only child, to Belott, who by 1604 had completed his apprenticeship and was working for a fixed salary in the groundfloor shop. But he held back, and Madame Mountjoy 'did send and persuade one Master Shakespeare that lay in the house to persuade the plaintiff to the same marriage'. The dramatist conveyed to Belott the father's promises with respect to the marriage portion, and also the information that, should he refuse the match, 'she should never cost him, the defendant her father, a groat. Whereupon, and in regard Master Shakespeare had told them that they should have a sum of money for a portion from the father, they were made sure by Master Shakespeare by giving their consent, and agreed to marry...' Thus deposed Daniel Nicholas, friend and neighbour of the Mountjoys. The wedding took place at St Olave's church on 19 March 1604. Later Belott quarrelled with his father-in-law over the dowry and a promised legacy; hence the suit. In his testimony Shakespeare, described as a gentleman of Stratford-upon-Avon, remembered the plaintiff as an apprentice who 'did well and honestly behave himself', and the defendant as one who showed 'great good will and affection towards the said complainant'. But the crucial points – the amount of the portion and when it was to be paid – Shakespeare could not recall, nor could he remember what Mountjoy had promised his daughter after his decease. The court referred the case to the elders of the French church in London for arbitration.

No records exist to connect the playwright's wife and family with any of his residences in the capital; presumably they awaited his visits to Stratford. According to Aubrey, 'Master William Shakespeare was wont to go into Warwickshire once a year.' Unlike Greene, he did not sever himself from his provincial roots, but instead carefully nurtured over the years his connection with the town of his birth. There he bought houses and land, and engaged in other dealings with the inhabitants: loans, sales, negotiations, and suits. These transactions testify to his prominence in the life of Stratford.

In 1597 he purchased the Great House of New Place. Three storeys high and with five gables (in the sketch, recently recovered, made from memory by the eighteenth-century artist Vertue), it had a frontage of sixty feet on Chapel Street and a depth of seventy feet along Chapel Lane. The second largest dwelling in Stratford, New Place became Shakespeare's permanent residence until his death. In the seventeenth century the garden was noted for its grapevines, and there, tradition holds, Shakespeare planted with his own hands a mulberry tree; it eventually became the source of a ceaseless stream of curios and relics. The family seems to have moved into the house in 1597, for early the next year a survey of the Chapel Street Ward showed Shakespeare as owning ten quarters (or eighty bushels) of corn and malt. In January 1599 he sold the Stratford Corporation a load of stone perhaps left over from the repair of the Great House.

No sooner had he bought the property than Shakespeare was open to other real-estate investments. 'It seemeth,' wrote Abraham Sturley on 24 January 1598 to Richard Quiney in London, '...that our countryman Master Shakspere is willing to disburse some money upon some odd yardland or other at Shottri or near about us.' This same Quiney, whose father had served together with John Shakespeare on Corporation business, wrote on 25 October the only extant letter to the poet. Addressed 'To my loving good friend and countryman Master William Shackespere', it requests a loan of £30 to help Quiney with his London debts. The fact that the letter was discovered among the Quiney papers suggests that it was never delivered.

On 1 May 1602 Shakespeare bought a large tract, 107 acres of arable land plus 20 acres of pasture, in Old Stratford, a farming area about a mile and a half north of town. For this freehold estate he paid William and John Combe the substantial sum of £320 in cash. That month the poet also bought a cottage (perhaps to lodge a servant) and a quarter of an acre of land on the south side of Chapel Lane, facing the garden of New Place. Three years later, on 24 July 1605, Shakespeare invested £440 in the purchase of a half interest in the lease of tithes on 'corn, grain, blade, and hay' from Old Stratford, Welcombe, and Bishopton, and on 'wool, lambs, and other small and privy tithes' from Stratford parish; he also agreed to pay rents totalling £22 a year, and to collect – or have collected – the tithes himself. They brought him a net income of £60 per annum.

In 1608 Shakespeare sued John Addenbrooke, gentleman, for a debt of £6 in the Stratford court of record. The same bench had heard his complaint, a few years previously, against Shakespeare's neighbour, Philip Rogers, who had bought from him twenty bushels of malt and borrowed 2s. but had repaid only 6s. of the entire debt. Such litigation is commonplace in the period.

In the last two years of his life Shakespeare was involved (although not very deeply) in a fierce debate over enclosure in the Welcombe area, where lay some of his tithe holdings. Several landholders in the neighbourhood urged the enclosure, which would have combined the narrow strips of cultivated soil into larger units surrounded by fences. If more productive agriculture resulted, Shakespeare would have stood to gain; if, on the other hand, the scheme involved converting arable land into pasture, he would have been placed at a disadvantage. What his views on the question were, we do not know; possibly he favoured enclosure. Late in 1614 Thomas Greene, his cousin who was the town clerk of Stratford and a tithe holder opposing the plan, sounded out some of the leading citizens, among them Shakespeare, whose name appears in Greene's memoranda. On 23 December he noted: 'Letters written: one to Master Manneryng, another to Master Shakespeare, with almost all the Company's hands to either. I also writ of myself to my cousin Shakspeare the copies of all our oaths made; then also a note of the inconveniences would grow by the enclosure...'

Shakespeare's portfolio of real-estate investments included one made in London. On 10 November 1613 he sealed a deed for the purchase of the Blackfriars Gate-house from Henry Walker, 'citizen and minstrel of London', for £140. The next day Shakespeare mortgaged the property back to Walker for £60; apparently £80 was paid down in cash, with the mortgage a security for the remainder. So far as we can gather, the dramatist bought the house, which stood close by to the Blackfriars Theatre, as a speculation rather than for use as a dwelling. He had by then retired to Stratford, and made only occasional visits to London.

Thus, during the middle years of his career, while he was becoming the most popular playwright of the London stage, Shakespeare maintained his ties with Stratford and built an estate that he would pass on to his heirs. Meanwhile, the cycle of birth and marriage and death went on. The parish register of Holy Trinity records, on 11 August 1596, the burial of Hamnet Shakespeare at the age of eleven. John Shakespeare died in September 1601; his widow survived him for seven years. The poet's favourite daughter Susanna married John Hall on 5 June 1607. A Stratford physician, he won (we are told) 'great fame for his skill, far and near'. Perhaps the pair lived for a time at the handsome house in Old Town, near the church, known today as Hall's Croft; after Shakespeare's death they took up residence at New Place. They had one child, Elizabeth, christened 21 February 1608. Shakespeare's younger daughter Judith did not marry until 1616, when she was thirty-one. She took for her husband Thomas Quiney, son of the Richard who had sought to borrow money from the poet in 1598.

A vintner whose character was not exemplary, Thomas set up shop, shortly after the wedding, at The Cage, a house at the corner of High Street and Bridge Street in Stratford. They had three children, all born after Shakespeare's death.

One January, either in 1615 or 1616, when he was still 'in perfect health and memory', Shakespeare drew up his last will and testament. Later, after Judith's wedding, he called in his lawyer Francis Collins (who had previously represented him in some of his business transactions) to make revisions. This was on 25 March, and by then Shakespeare's health was failing: he signed in a quavering hand, and he could not recall the name of one of his three nephews – the solicitor had to leave a blank space.

In his will Shakespeare provided for his survivors. To the poor of Stratford he left £10. He remembered local friends: William Reynolds, Anthony Nash, and his brother John Nash. Thomas Combe, whose rich and usurious uncle had bequeathed the poet £5, received his sword; to his lifelong friend Hamnet Sadler he gave money to buy a memorial ring. Nor did Shakespeare overlook his London colleagues of the days with the King's men, but left sums for rings to Richard Burbage, John Heminges, and Henry Condell; they would not forget him. His sole remaining sister, Mrs Joan Hart, was allowed to stay for the rest of her life in the Henley Street homestead, and was given £20 in cash and the testator's wearing apparel. Her three sons received £5 each. A godson, William Walker, aged eight, was left 20s. in gold. To his daughter Judith, Shakespeare bequeathed his broad silver-gilt bowl, £100 as a dowry and another £50 for relinquishing her interest in the cottage on Chapel Lane; also an additional £150, provided 'she or any issue of her body be living at the end of three years next ensuing the day of this my will'.

The Halls, whom he designated as his executors, figure most prominently in the instrument. Their eight-year-old daughter Elizabeth received Shakespeare's plate. The bulk of the estate went to Susanna:

All that capital messuage or tenements with the appurtenances, in Stratford aforesaid, called the New Place, wherein I now dwell, and two messuages or tenements with the appurtenances situate, lying, and being in Henley Street within the borough of Stratford aforesaid; and all my barns, stables, orchards, gardens, lands, tenements, and hereditaments whatsoever, situate ...within the towns, hamlets, villages, fields, and grounds of Stratford-upon-Avon, Old Stratford, Bushopton, and Welcombe, or in any of them in the said county of Warwick. And also all that messuage or tenement with the appurtenances wherein one John Robinson dwelleth, situate...in the Blackfriars in London near the Wardrobe; and all other my lands, tenements, and hereditaments whatsoever.

After her decease the entailed estate was to go to her eldest surviving son, and then to that son's male heirs, and (in default of such issue) to the male heirs of Shakespeare's younger daughter. Thus he sought to keep from dissolution the substantial estate that with toil and shrewd investment he had over the years assembled. But his intention was frustrated. Susanna bore no male children; Judith's three sons died young; Shakespeare's four grandchildren left no issue. Eventually the property passed to strangers.

Anne Shakespeare is mentioned once in an interlineation, apparently inserted in the will as an afterthought: 'Item, I give unto my wife my second best bed with the furniture,' that is, with the hangings, bed linen, etc. This clause has given rise to endless and often heated controversy over the poet's domestic felicity or lack of it. 'His wife had not wholly escaped his memory,' wrote the great Edmond Malone in the eighteenth century: 'he had forgot her, – he had recollected her, – but so recollected her, as more strongly to mark how little he esteemed her; he had already (as is vulgarly expressed) cut her off, not indeed with a shilling, but with an old bed.' His comment influenced opinion for a long period, but eventually it was pointed out (by Charles Knight in the nineteenth century) that the law entitled a widow to one third of her husband's estate, and that there was no need to mention this disposition in the will. The significance of the bequest can only be guessed, but possibly the bed carried sentimental associations, the best bed being reserved for guests at New Place.

On 23 April 1616 Shakespeare died. About his last illness we have no certain information, although half a century later the vicar of Holy Trinity, John Ward, noted in his diary a story that must then have had currency in Stratford: 'Shakespear, Drayton, and Ben Jhonson had a merry meeting, and it seems drank too hard, for Shakespear died of a fever there contracted.' This story has some plausibility – Jonson enjoyed his cup, and Drayton, who haled from Warwickshire, frequently visited the nearby village of Clifford Chambers. Judith Shakespeare's wedding may have provided the occasion for conviviality. But the anecdote is no more than that; medically it seems dubious, and as a gossip Ward is not entirely reliable.

On the twenty-fifth Shakespeare was laid to rest; so the parish register records. As a notable son of Stratford, he was buried within the chancel of Holy Trinity; more ordinary citizens, including his mother and father, were laid to rest in the churchyard. On the flagstone of the dramatist's grave appears this malediction:

> Good friend, for Jesus' sake forbear
> To dig the dust enclosed here!
> Bless'd be the man that spares these stones,
> And curs'd be he that moves my bones.

We do not know whether Shakespeare himself composed these lines, which are directed not to casual visitors to the church but to the sexton, who sometimes had to disturb the dead in order to make room for a new grave.

Within several years of the interment there was erected, to honour Shakespeare's memory, a monument in the north wall of the chancel, near the grave. A half-length bust of the poet is framed by a niched arch; a pen in his right hand, he is in the act of creation. Above the arch is emblazoned in bas-relief the familiar coat of arms, as described in 1596 by the College of Heralds: 'Gold, on a bend sables, a spear of the first steeled argent; and for his crest or cognisance a falcon, his wings displayed argent, steeled as aforesaid, set upon a helmet with mantels and tassels...' (The words 'non sanz droict', appearing above the trick of coat and crest in two drafts of a Heralds' document, are taken to represent the family motto, but we have no evidence of their use as such by Shakespeare or his heirs.) Small nude figures representing Rest and Labour sit on either side of the arms; a skull forms the apex of the triangular design. The stonemason who carved the monument was Gheerart Janssen, of Dutch origin, whose shop stood in Southwark, a short distance from the Globe. The dramatist and his colleagues perhaps knew it.

In 1623 Heminges and Condell honoured Shakespeare with a monument of another kind by collecting and publishing his plays. They dedicated the volume to the Earls of Pembroke and Montgomery, who, we are told, showed the author much favour while he lived; William Herbert, third Earl of Pembroke, would become a leading contender for the role of the Sweet Boy of the Sonnets, which had been published in 1609 with a dedication to 'Mr W. H.'. On the title-page of the Folio appears a clumsy portrait of Shakespeare engraved by Martin Droeshout; this likeness is commended by Jonson in a verse on the adjoining flyleaf. (The Droeshout portrait and the Stratford bust constitute the only authoritative representations of the poet, although claims have been made for many others, most notably the Chandos painting.) In their preface addressed 'To the Great Variety of Readers', the editors comment on the habits of composition of their colleague: 'His mind and hand went together, and what he thought, he uttered with that easiness that we have scarce received from him a blot in his papers.' To which Jonson rejoined, in his *Timber: or, Discoveries*, 'Would he had blotted a thousand!' But in the fifth preliminary leaf to the Folio he paid noble tribute to the memory of his beloved, the sweet swan of Avon who was not for an age but for all time. Another encomium came from the pen of Leonard Digges, a University College, Oxford, scholar, who was the stepson of Thomas Russell, a Warwickshire squire appointed by Shakespeare as one of the overseers of his will.

The claim of Heminges and Condell that Shakespeare never blotted a line invites scepticism (we know that he revised), but we do not doubt them when they describe their editorial task as a labour of love, designed 'without ambition either of self-profit or fame; only to keep the memory of so worthy a friend and fellow alive, as was our Shakespeare'. Apart from Greene, none of his contemporaries seems to have uttered a malicious word about Shakespeare. Chettle, as we have seen, praised his civil demeanour and uprightness of dealing. From others we hear of good Will, sweet Shakespeare, friendly Shakespeare, so dear loved a neighbour. The actor Augustine Phillips in 1605 remembered him in his will and bequeathed him a thirty shilling piece in gold. Praise did not come easily to Jonson, but in his *Discoveries*, when not under eulogistic obligations, he confessed that he loved the man and honoured his memory on this side idolatry: 'He was indeed honest, and of an open and free nature; had an excellent fancy, brave notions, and gentle expressions.' Aubrey wrote more than half a century after Shakespeare's death, and so his jottings belong to the mythos rather than to the factual record, but we are not inclined to distrust him when he notes, 'He was a handsome well-shaped man, very good company, and of a very ready and pleasant smooth wit.'

Shakespeare's widow lived to see the installation of the monument in Holy Trinity, but not the publication of the First Folio. She died on 6 August 1623. A tradition holds that she 'did earnestly desire to be laid in the same tomb' with her husband, but the injunction against opening the grave prevailed, and she was instead placed alongside. John Hall died in 1635 and his wife in 1649. They too lie in the chancel near the poet. Judith Quiney died in 1662, and Shakespeare's last surviving grandchild, Lady Bernard, in February 1670. New Place, bequeathed to the Bernards by her will, was rebuilt in 1702 and razed in 1759.

2

THE PLAYHOUSES AND THE STAGE

RICHARD HOSLEY

It is convenient to begin this chapter with a brief enquiry into the kinds of temporary playhouse and stage that existed in England on the eve of construction of the first permanent Elizabethan playhouse – that is to say, about 1575. By that time the old medieval stage of Place-and-scaffolds, still in use in Scotland early in the sixteenth century, had fallen into disuse; and the stage of the pageant-wagons, though it would be used in secular contexts until the early seventeenth century, had arrived at the end of its long career as the stage of the great medieval Corpus Christi cycles. Thus the kind of temporary stage that was dominant in England about 1575 was the booth stage of the marketplace – a small rectangular stage mounted on trestles or barrels and 'open' in the sense of being surrounded by spectators on three sides (Fig. 1).

The stage proper of the booth stage generally measured from 15 to 25 ft. in width and from 10 to 15 ft. in depth; its height above the ground averaged about 5 ft. 6 in., with extremes ranging as low as 4 ft. and as high as 8 ft.; and it was backed by a cloth-covered booth, usually open at the top, which served as a tiring-house (mimorum aedes). In typical small examples the booth proper employed four upright posts joined at the top by horizontal poles or timbers, so that the whole booth was constructed as a single bay and the booth front, accordingly, consisted of a single opening in which curtains were hung. In larger examples six or eight or even ten uprights were used, so that the booth was constructed in two or three or even four bays and the booth front, accordingly, consisted of two or three or even four openings in which curtains were hung. The booth stage did not usually employ a 'containing' barrier or playhouse – though because of the lack of such a means of controlling access to the performance the collection of money constituted rather a problem; occasionally, as in the late fifteenth-century morality play *Mankind*, the performance would be stopped briefly at an exciting moment while money was collected from the spectators. But growth in the size of audiences and the experience of having performed in 'rounds' enclosed by a fence or an earthwork 'hill' apparently led the players to investigate ways of controlling access to the performance and thus of collecting charges for admission more efficiently. About 1575 there were two kinds of building in England, both designed for functions other than the acting of plays, which were adapted by the players as temporary outdoor playhouses.

Fig. 1. A booth stage set up in a marketplace

One was the animal-baiting ring or 'game house' (beargarden or bull ring), examples of which are recorded in pictorial and other records as standing on the south bank of the Thames opposite the City of London in the 1560s. The early Bankside baiting-houses were round wooden amphitheatres consisting of (probably) two galleries super-imposed one above the other and defining a circular 'pit' some 60 or more feet in diameter. We have no record of the use of a baiting-house for the performance of plays, but the close physical resemblance between the baiting-houses and later 'public' playhouses makes the hypothesis of such use a defensible one. (Compare the later daily alterna-tion of animal-baiting with play-acting in the Hope Playhouse or

Fourth Beargarden of 1614.) Presumably a booth stage was set up against the inner circle of the baiting-house frame, an audience standing in the pit collected around the three sides of the stage, and an additional audience, corresponding to spectators in upper-storey windows of houses in the marketplace situation, watched the performance from seats in the galleries (Fig. 2). Both pit and gallery spectators would, of course, upon entrance to the 'house', have paid fees for the privilege of viewing the performance.

The other kind of building was the inn – or, rather, that particular kind of 'great inn' which consisted of a group of adjoining buildings arranged usually in a rectangular plan so as to define an enclosed 'yard'. Use of inn-yards for the performance of plays is indicated by (among other records) the Act of Common Council of the City of London in 1574 restraining innkeepers and others from permitting plays to be performed 'within the house-yard or any other place within the liberties of this City'. Like the animal-baiting house, the inn-yard constituted a 'natural' playhouse: presumably a booth stage was set up against a wall at one side of the yard (usually one of the 'long' sides), an audience standing in the yard surrounded the stage on three sides, an additional audience observed the performance from seats in windows and galleries overlooking the yard, and, most important, the price of admission was gathered at the moment of each spectator's entrance to the 'house' (Fig. 3).

In one respect the inn-yard may have constituted a better playhouse than the animal-baiting house: if paved, a given yard, unlike the necessarily unpaved pit of the baiting-house, would have afforded protection against the miring of standing spectators during or following wet weather. (Opportunities for an older pastime than the viewing of plays – implied by the reference to 'chambers and secret places' in the Act of Common Council of 1574 – would also have been superior.) But it seems clear that in at least three respects the baiting-house must have been superior to the inn-yard as a playhouse: usually its pit was considerably greater in area than the yard of an inn, it was 'round' instead of rectangular in ground plan (hence more efficient in the accommodation of both pit and gallery spectators), and it had galleries that entirely surrounded the pit as opposed to a gallery here and there and occasional windows overlooking the yard of the usual inn. In this respect it is significant that, in the permanent playhouse constructed in 'the great yard' of the Boar's Head Inn in London in 1598, galleries were apparently built around the four sides of the yard.[1]

The booth stage was essentially an outdoor stage, and the temporary playhouse that accommodated it in a baiting-house or an inn-yard was, despite the location of part of the audience in roofed galleries or upper-storey rooms of an inn, essentially an outdoor playhouse. What was the situation when, during the century ending about 1575, the players performed indoors – in guildhalls, schools or colleges, inns of court, manor houses, palaces, churches, inns, and elsewhere? In most instances what the players did was to convert a domestic (or public) hall into a temporary indoor playhouse. There is some reason to believe that they occasionally set up a booth stage against one wall of the hall in question, and such practice is recorded pictorially in France

Fig. 2. A booth stage set up in the pit of an animal-baiting house

or Italy in the *Andria* illustrations of the Lyons Terence of 1493 – most notably in the frontispiece and the illustration for the opening scene of that play. It also seems probable, however, that English players performing in a hall would generally have preferred to use the already existing 'screens' passage as a tiring-house. In part because of the customary placement of the high table on the dais at the 'upper' end of a hall, plays were normally performed at the 'lower' end – either upon the hall floor or upon a low stage set up against the hall screen (or upon both). At this period the domestic hall screen was normally equipped with two doorways, and these, being without doors, were covered with hangings in order to exclude draughts from the hall. Thus the players, in most situations in which they might undertake to perform a play indoors, found ready at hand, without the necessity

Fig. 3. A booth stage set up in an inn-yard

of preparation, that indispensable convenience of booth-stage production, a pair of curtained entranceways to the playing-area (in this case the hall floor or a low stage set up against the hall screen or both). In a majority of halls, furthermore, use of the screens passage as a tiring-house afforded the players the secondary convenience of a musicians' gallery directly over the passage which could, at need, be put to occasional use as an 'upper station' for the performance of action at an upper-storey window or upon the walls of a town or castle (Fig. 4).

It is customary to distinguish two major classes of permanent Elizabethan playhouse, 'public' and 'private'. The terms are somewhat cloudy, but what they designate is clear enough. In general, the public playhouses were large, 'round', outdoor theatres, whereas the private

Fig. 4. A performance on the floor of a theatrically unmodified domestic hall

playhouses were smaller, rectangular, indoor theatres. (An exception among public playhouses in the matter of roundness was the square Fortune of 1600.) The maximum capacity of a typical public playhouse (the Swan or the Globe) was about 3,000 spectators; that of a typical private playhouse (the Second Blackfriars or the Phoenix), about 700 spectators. At the public playhouses a majority of spectators stood in the yard for a penny (the remainder sitting in galleries and boxes for twopence or more), whereas at the private playhouses all spectators were seated (in pit, galleries, and boxes) and paid sixpence or more. Originally the private playhouses were used exclusively by Boys' companies, but this distinction disappeared about 1609 when the

King's men began using the Blackfriars in winter as well as the Globe in summer. Originally also the private playhouses were found only within the City of London (the Paul's Playhouse, the First and Second Blackfriars), the public playhouses only in the suburbs (the Theatre, the Curtain, the Rose, the Globe, the Fortune, the Red Bull); but this distinction disappeared about 1606 with the opening of the Whitefriars Playhouse to the west of Ludgate. Public-theatre audiences, though socially heterogeneous, were drawn mainly from the lower classes – a situation that has caused modern scholars to refer to the public-theatre audiences as 'popular'; whereas private-theatre audiences tended to be better educated and of higher social rank – 'select' is the word most usually opposed to 'popular' in this respect. Finally, the taste of the audience varied considerably in the two kinds of playhouse, and so accordingly, to a degree, did the kind of play presented.[2]

It has been suggested convincingly that the word *private*, as used by publishers on the title-pages of plays, was designed 'to increase their sales by advertising the fact that the play was of the sophisticated kind written for the indoor theatres', the term merely connoting 'a degree of exclusiveness and superiority'.[3] Thus the opposed term *public* may be interpreted as referring to a playhouse of the outdoor variety that lacked the 'exclusiveness and superiority' of the indoor playhouses. Examples are afforded by Dekker in *The Gull's Hornbook* (1609): 'Whether, therefore, the gatherers of the *public* or *private* playhouse stand to receive the afternoon's rent,...'

It should be recognized, however, that the terms *public* and *private* were used also (as one would perhaps expect) in their more usual senses. Thus we find that Heywood's *Love's Mistress* is advertised on its title-page (1636) as having been '*publicly* acted...at the Phoenix', Chapman's *Charles Duke of Byron* (1625) as having been acted 'at the Blackfriars and other *public* stages' – both playhouses, of course, being 'private' in the earlier defined sense of that word. This secondary (but more basic) sense of the term *public* is illustrated, about 1619, in a complaint by residents of the Blackfriars precinct against the Second Blackfriars: 'the owner of the said playhouse doth under the name of a *private* house (respecting indeed private commodity only) convert the said house to a *public* playhouse, unto which there is daily such resort of people,...' Clearly the term *public* here refers to a playhouse that anyone might attend by virtue of paying the price of admission. The term *open* is apparently a synonym, as on the title-page of Edwards's *Damon and Pythias* (1571), which contemplates performance of that play 'either in *private* or *open* audience'.

Correspondingly, the term *private* in the Blackfriars complaint refers to a playhouse that one might attend only by virtue of belonging to a 'closed' society. Thus the title-page of *The First Two Comedies of Terence* (1627) states that the comedies in question are 'fitted for scholars' *private* action in their schools'. This sense is implied also in the title-page statement (1629) that Carlell's *Deserving Favourite* has been performed 'first before the King's Majesty [i.e. at Court, or *privately*], and since *publicly* at the Blackfriars'. The term was used also in this sense in the Act of Common Council of 1574 in excluding from its ban on performances within the City of London the performance of plays 'in the *private* house, dwelling, or lodging of any nobleman, citizen, or gentleman,...without public or common collection of money of the auditory or beholders thereof'. If, however, visitors were present at a performance given before a usually 'closed' society, the performance, though essentially 'private', could be described as 'public'. Thus in 1605 at St John's College, Oxford, *The Tragedy of Lucretia* was '*publicly* acted...with good commendation and diverse strangers entertained in respect thereof'.

Although both the baiting-house and the inn-yard were used as temporary playhouses before creation of the first permanent Eliza-bethan playhouse, it seems likely that the physical form of the public playhouse originated mainly in the animal-baiting house. (It is possible, of course, that the rectangular shape of the inn-yard may have been an influence upon the square Fortune.) In accordance with this theory we may suppose that James Burbage, when he built the Theatre in 1576, merely adapted the form of the baiting-house to theatrical needs. To do so he built a large round structure very much like a baiting-house but with five major innovations in the received form. First (though not necessarily immediately), he paved the ring with brick or stone, thus transforming what had been an unpaved 'pit' into a paved 'yard'. In doing this his chief purpose would have been to make possible an efficient system of drains to carry off rainwater falling into the yard. Here his model, both for the thing itself and for its name, may have been the yard of a great inn or the courtyard of a great house or palace. Second, Burbage erected a stage in the yard. Here his model was the booth stage of the marketplace, built rather larger than any recorded example and, since a permanent structure, supported by posts rather than trestles or barrels. Third, Burbage erected a perma-nent tiring-house in place of the booth which had been set up in front of a few bays of the frame in the earlier temporary arrangement in an animal-baiting ring. Here his chief model was the screens passage of the Tudor domestic hall, modified to withstand the weather by the insertion of doors in the doorways. Presumably the tiring-house, as a permanent structure, was inset into the frame of the playhouse rather than, as in the older temporary situation of the booth stage, set up against the frame of a baiting-house. Thus Burbage produced a structure which, when the leaves of the doors had been opened outward through an arc of 180° and hangings placed in or in front of the open doorways, reproduced that indispensable convenience of the booth stage, a pair of curtained entranceways to the stage; and the gallery over the tiring-house (presumably divided into boxes) was capable of serving variously as a 'Lord's room' for privileged or high-paying spectators, as a music-room, and as a station for the occasional performance of action 'above'. Fourth, Burbage built a 'cover' over the rear part of the stage, supported by posts rising from the yard and surmounted by a 'hut'. The precise origin of such a 'stage superstructure' is difficult to identify, but it must have been designed primarily to house suspension-gear for flying-effects, and such gear had been used in the English street theatre as early as the end of the fourteenth century. And, fifth, Burbage added a third gallery to the frame, for the original Bankside baiting-houses (as recorded in the 'Agas' View of London) appear to have been two-storey buildings. Here Burbage may have been influenced only by normal business acumen, but any of a number of three-storeyed architectural forms might have served as his model.

The theory of origin and development suggested in the preceding paragraph accords with our chief pictorial source of information about the Elizabethan stage, the 'De Wit' drawing of the interior of the Swan Playhouse (c. 1596; Fig. 5). This shows a round playhouse frame constructed apparently in 24 bays and measuring presumably about 96 ft. in diameter.[4] Thus the playhouse would have been large enough to accommodate an audience of some 3,000 spectators (the figure given in the notes accompanying the drawing). The playhouse frame, consisting of three galleries superimposed one above the other, defines a circular yard some 70 ft. in diameter. At one side of the playhouse yard is a large rectangular stage (*proscaenium*) which extends to about the middle of the yard. The stage is depicted as deeper than wide, but the depiction is probably a distortion in the drawing, for numerous considerations suggest that the stage was wider than deep. The actual size of the stage depends on a number of variable factors: the diameter of the playhouse frame, the depth of the frame, the number of bays of the frame, and the degree of projection of the stage into the yard. In the present case, assuming a 24-sided playhouse frame with an outer diameter of 96 ft., a frame 12 ft. 6 in. deep, and a projection of the stage as far as the middle of the playhouse yard, we may estimate the Swan stage as 43 ft. in width and about 27 ft. in depth (dimensions in a ratio of about 8:5). The height of the stage may be conjectured as 5 ft. 6 in., about the average height of the booth stage.

At the back of the stage in the Swan drawing is a 'tiring-house' (*mimorum aedes*) which appears to project considerably from the playhouse frame but which, in actuality, may have projected only a foot or two. The tiring-house is equipped, in the first storey, with two large, round-headed, double-hung doors opening out upon the stage and, in the second storey, with a row of six windows which are presumably the openings of boxes of a 'Lord's room over the stage' (to quote Jonson's allusion in *Every Man out of His Humour*). If the Swan tiring-house was about 40 ft. long, each of the tiring-house doors in the drawing may be estimated as about 7 ft. 6 in. wide and about 9 ft. high; and each of the windows of the gallery over the stage as about 6 ft. square.

In the Swan drawing two large columns in the Corinthian mode rise from the stage (and, of course, from the yard below) to support a 'cover' or 'shadow' or 'heavens' which, running the full length of the tiring-house at the level of its third storey, extends forward from the tiring-house so as to lie directly over the rear part of the stage. And immediately above the stage cover, at the level of what would be a fourth storey of the tiring-house, is a 'hut'. Presumably the fourth-storey hut housed suspension-gear for flying-effects and the third-storey stage cover served as a loading-room for players preparing to 'fly' down to the stage.

The theory of origin and development suggested above accords also with our two chief verbal sources of information about the Elizabethan stage, the builder's contracts for the Fortune (1599) and the Hope (1613).[5] Both contracts call for a three-storey playhouse frame, and the Fortune contract specifies the height of each of the three storeys of the frame: in ascending order, 12 ft., 11 ft., and 9 ft. The Fortune contract also states that the stage in that playhouse is to be 43 ft. wide and that it should 'extend to the middle of the yard'. Thus, since the contract gives the dimensions of the yard as 55 ft. square, the depth of the stage is required to be 27 ft. 6 in., and the dimensions of the stage are in a ratio of about 8:5.

The theory accords also with our second most important pictorial source of information about the Elizabethan stage, Wenzel Hollar's pen-and-ink sketch (*c.* 1640) for his Long Bird's-Eye View of London (1647). The sketch (like the engraving that in part derives from it) depicts a round Second Globe and Hope, both equipped with the exterior stair-towers which the Hope contract requires at that playhouse on the analogy of the stair-towers at the Swan. Presumably such exterior stair-towers, whether roofed and enclosed as shown by Hollar or unroofed and open, already existed in the animal-baiting houses of about 1575 and were taken over from them by Burbage when he constructed the Theatre in 1576.

Fig. 5. The 'De Wit' drawing of the Swan Playhouse

The Fortune contract calls for a square playhouse measuring 80 ft. on a side. All the other public playhouses appear to have been 'round' – that is to say, constructed to a ground plan in the shape of a polygon having a large number of sides. Apparently the Swan was constructed in 24 bays, and 24 sides would be an appropriate number if the Swan measured 96 ft. in diameter since in that case the length of horizontal timbers in the outer and inner faces of the frame (12 ft. 6 in. and 9 ft. 3 in., respectively) would have been of convenient length for transportation and handling in construction. That the Swan was at least 96 ft. in diameter is suggested by De Wit's statement that the playhouse could accommodate 3,000 spectators. De Wit's figure has occasionally been scouted as too large, but it is confirmed by the statement of the Spanish ambassador, apropos of Middleton's *Game at Chess* at the Second Globe in 1624, that more than 12,000 people witnessed performances of that play during the first four days of its extraordinary run of 'nine days together'; he says also that more than 3,000 persons were present on the day that the audience was smallest. Presumably, then, it was common knowledge that such playhouses as the Swan and the Second Globe could accommodate a capacity crowd of about 3,000 spectators.

The question arises whether the size of the Swan was typical of Elizabethan public playhouses. An answer is suggested by the general similarity in size of five of the public playhouses. According to its builder's contract, the Hope, built in 1613–14, was to be of 'such large compass, form, wideness, and height as the playhouse called the Swan', built almost twenty years earlier in 1595. Hence we have a class of two playhouses, the Swan and the Hope, which were of the same size. Again, the Second Globe was built in 1614 'upon an old foundation'. Since this would be the foundation of the First Globe, built fifteen years earlier in 1599 and destroyed by fire in 1613, we may suppose that the Second Globe was of the same size as the First. Moreover, the First Globe, as is well known, was constructed of the dismantled timbers of the Theatre. Since the timbers would presumably (through attention to 'carpenter's marks') have been reassembled in their original relationships so as to take advantage of the original cutting and jointing,[6] we may suppose that the First Globe, built in 1599, was of the same size as the Theatre, built some twenty-five years earlier in 1576. It follows that the Second Globe of 1614 was also of the same size as the Theatre of 1576. Hence we have a second class, composed of three playhouses, the Theatre, the First Globe, and the Second Globe, which were of the same size. And the two classes of playhouse were themselves of approximately the same size, for the reason that one theatre from the first class (the Swan) and another from the second (the Second Globe) were independently described as capable of accommodating about 3,000 spectators. All told, the evidence seems hospitable to a theory that most of the round public playhouses – specifically, the Theatre (1576), the Swan (1595), the First Globe (1599), the Hope (1614), and the Second Globe (1614) – were of about the same size.

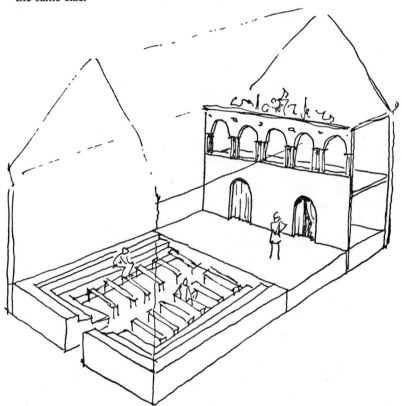

Fig. 6. A reconstruction of a small private playhouse such as the early Paul's or the First Blackfriars

It seems likely that the physical form of the Elizabethan private playhouse originated mainly in the Tudor domestic hall. In accordance with this theory we may suppose that Sebastian Westcott, when he built the unnamed theatre of the Paul's Boys in or shortly before 1575, merely adapted a small hall connected with St Paul's Church to theatrical needs. To do so he may have made only one major innovation, the construction of a low stage (perhaps 4 ft. high) running across the hall from one wall to the other immediately in front of the hall screen. The stage, if the containing hall were (let us say) 26 ft. wide, would have been 26 ft. in width and, presumably, about 16 ft. 6 in. in depth (dimensions in a ratio of about 8:5). The screens passage, if surmounted by a musicians' gallery, could have served without adaptation as a tiring-house, it being possible to fit up hangings in the two doorways, and the 'gallery over the stage' being available for occasional action 'above'; or a gallery, if lacking, could readily have been added to the original one-storey screen. Three tiring-house doors, if desired, could have been provided by the expedient of converting the central panel of the screen into a middle doorway. Westcott might then have completed his theatrical arrangements by merely running benches across the remainder of the hall floor from wall to wall, by setting up ground 'degrees' around a narrow section of floor containing benches (Fig. 6), or by constructing shallow galleries around a narrow 'pit' containing benches.

Nothing is known about the dimensions of the hall (or even the very identity of the hall) in which the Paul's Playhouse was presumably housed. In the case, however, of the First Blackfriars Playhouse, constructed by Richard Farrant in 1576, we are on slightly firmer ground, since we know that the hall in question, an upper-storey room of the Old Buttery of the Dominican Priory of London, was 26 ft. wide. (The building was 95 ft. long, but presumably only part of this length was used for the playhouse.) Thus the general arrangement of the First Blackfriars was presumably much the same as that suggested for the Paul's Playhouse.

In the case of the Second Blackfriars Playhouse of 1596 we have very considerable information, chiefly in the form of verbal records giving dimensions. The designer was James Burbage, and he built his playhouse in the upper-storey Parliament Chamber of the Upper Frater of the priory. The Parliament Chamber measured 100 ft. in length, but for the playhouse Burbage used only two-thirds of this length. The room in question, after the removal of partitions dividing it into apartments, measured 46 ft. in width and 66 ft. in length. In order to convert this room into a playhouse, Burbage made, according to a recently proposed reconstruction,[7] four major innovations. First, since a hall screen (if there was one) could hardly have survived the compartmentation of the Parliament Chamber into apartments earlier in the sixteenth century, he built, at one end of the room, a tiring-house modelled either directly on the screens passage of a Tudor domestic hall or on a tiring-house itself modelled on such a screens passage. The tiring-house, running the full width of the hall, was thus 46 ft.

long and perhaps 12 ft. deep (including the thickness of the tiring-house wall). Probably there were three doorways in the tiring-house façade; in the reconstruction they are given as 7 ft. wide and 9 ft. tall. The second storey of the tiring-house would have been a 'gallery over the stage', the three boxes of which might have been used variously as

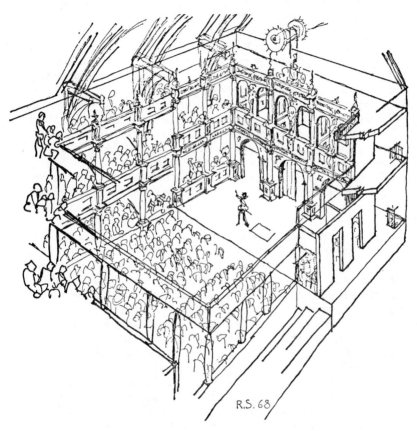

Fig. 7. A reconstruction of the Second Blackfriars

a Lord's room, as a music-room, and as an upper station for the occasional performance of action above. Second, Burbage built a low stage (perhaps 4 ft. 6 in. high) running across the hall from one wall to the other immediately in front of the tiring-house. Third, he built galleries around the three remaining sides of the room, thus defining a 'pit' which, if the galleries were 8 ft. 6 in. deep, would have measured

29 ft. in width and 27 ft. in depth. Presumably the pit was unraked. If the walls of the Parliament Chamber extended 32 ft. above the floor, space would have been available for three galleries (the top gallery perhaps unroofed), and presumably Burbage would have continued these across the stage to join the tiring-house, thus creating upper side-boxes over the stage and side-stage boxes at stage level. Accordingly the stage would have measured 29 ft. in width and 18 ft. 6 in. in depth (dimensions in a ratio of about 8:5). And, fourth, Burbage cut a trap door in the ceiling of the Parliament Chamber so as to make possible descents by suspension-gear housed in one of the 'rooms over the hall'. The proposed reconstruction is illustrated in the accompanying drawing by Richard Southern (Fig. 7).

The theory of origin and development suggested in preceding paragraphs is confirmed by a major pictorial source of information about the Elizabethan indoor playhouse. This is the set of drawings (probably by Inigo Jones) preserved at Worcester College, Oxford.[8] The drawings show a playhouse in a rectangular building with an apsidal end. (The ground plan might be described as in the shape of a closed horse-shoe with parallel sides.) The building is approximately 51 ft. long and 37 ft. wide (interior measure). The tiring-house runs the full width of the building at the rectangular end. The tiring-house is thus 37 ft. long, and it is 11 ft. deep including the thickness of the tiring-house wall. The stage is about 23 ft. wide and 14 ft. deep (dimensions in a ratio of 8:5). The height of the stage above the floor is 4 ft. The galleries, running round the apsidal end of the building, are 8 ft. 6 in. deep. They define an apsidal-ended pit with an unraked floor. Continuation of the galleries across the stage to join the tiring-house has the effect of creating upper side-boxes over the stage and side-stage boxes at stage level. There are three doorways in the tiring-house façade. The second storey of the tiring-house is a gallery over the stage divided into three bays. The two side bays are apparently intended for audience since degrees for seating are indicated. The middle bay, fronted with an arched window, may be interpreted as a music-room, and presumably this served also, at need, as an upper station for the occasional performance of action above. The drawings make no provision for suspension-gear, but such gear could easily have been housed in the attic above the playhouse if a trap door were cut in the playhouse ceiling.

Two parts of the stage in a playhouse like the Swan or the Second Blackfriars require only the briefest comment. Suspension-gear was used for the flying down of a deity from the 'heavens' (Jupiter in *Cymbeline*) or for special lifting effects (heaving Antony aloft in *Antony and Cleopatra*[9]). Since the winch was stationary, descents and ascents were of the bucket-in-a-well variety, the descending or ascending player alighting at or taking off from a central point on the stage a few feet forward of the tiring-house façade. And the trap door was used as a pit (*Titus Andronicus*), a grave (*Hamlet*), or the entrance to a vault or the netherworld. There appears to have been but a single trap door, placed in the middle of the stage.

Fig. 8. Hangings fitted up along the tiring-house façade of a public playhouse such as the Swan or the Globe

31

Three other parts of the stage, since controversial, require more detailed discussion: the 'discovery-space', the upper station, and the music-room.

The discovery-space was generally an open tiring-house doorway within which curtains (Fig. 7), or in front of which hangings (Fig. 8), had been fitted up.[10] Thus the discovery-space was a foot or two deep, some 7 ft. wide, and about 9 ft. tall. The conception is dependent on three characteristics of the Elizabethan discovery. First, it was extremely rare, there being evidence for only about a dozen discoveries in the several hundred scenes of Shakespeare's thirty-eight plays. Typical examples are the discovery of the dead Horatio in Kyd's *Spanish Tragedy*, of the three caskets in *The Merchant of Venice*, of the sleeping Falstaff in *1 Henry IV*, of the 'statue' of Hermione in *The Winter's Tale*, and of Ferdinand and Miranda playing at chess in *The Tempest*. Second, the Elizabethan discovery is essentially a 'show' or disclosure (usually for the benefit of a character on stage) of a character or object invested with some special interest or significance. That is to say, the discovery-space curtains were not used, as curtains commonly are in the proscenium-arch theatre, as a device to permit the placement of stage-properties out of sight of the audience. In the Elizabethan theatre beds (*Othello*[11]), tables (*Henry VIII*), chairs containing 'sick' characters (*King Lear*), and other such properties were simply carried or drawn on stage at need by attendant players. And, third, the Elizabethan discovery did not involve movement in depth within the discovery-space, for the discovered player usually leaves the discovery-space and comes forward upon the stage immediately or shortly after being discovered.

The upper station was generally the space at the front of one of the boxes of the tiring-house gallery over the stage.[12] Thus the upper station was essentially a box-window which sometimes measured as much as 6 ft. in width. The conception is dependent on three characteristics of Elizabethan action above. First, it was relatively rare, there being evidence for only about three dozen actions above in Shakespeare's thirty-eight plays. Second, Elizabethan action above was essentially an 'appearance' of one character in an elevated place to another character in a place below. The usual situations are the window of a house overlooking the street (Brabantio and Iago in *Othello*) and the walls of a town or castle overlooking the space below (the King and Bolingbroke in *Richard II*). And, third, Elizabethan action above does not involve movement in depth within the upper station, for in most instances the player above remains framed in the window while in dialogue with the player below and sometimes, at the conclusion of that dialogue, descends by way of the tiring-house stairs to stage level and re-enters 'to' the player below.

Like the upper station, the Elizabethan music-room was generally one of the boxes of the second-storey gallery over the stage.[13] (The theory of a third-storey music-room is without foundation.) Presumably the playhouse custom of placing music above originated in use of the musicians' gallery over the screens passage of a domestic hall. In any case, the music room was early a standard appurtenance of the private playhouses, where act-intervals and inter-act music were customary from the beginning. A music-room was at first lacking in the public playhouses, since public-theatre performances did not originally employ act-intervals and inter-act music. (In such playhouses off-stage music was generally performed within the tiring-house at stage level.) About 1609, however, after the King's men had begun performing at the Blackfriars as well as at the Globe, the custom of inter-act music seems to have spread from the private to the public playhouses, and with it apparently came the custom of using one of the tiring-house boxes over the stage as a music-room – compare the requirement of '*a sad song in the music-room*' in Middleton's *Chaste Maid in Cheapside*, a Swan play of 1613. The music-room, whether in a private or a public playhouse, was normally curtained, presumably so that the musicians could be concealed from the audience during the action of the play but readily made visible to them during the performance of inter-act music. And occasionally the music-room curtains were used for a discovery above or otherwise employed, as in the King's spying from an upper-storey window in *Henry VIII*. It may be added that the theory of use of a music-room for action above is confirmed by Jasper Mayne's praise of Ben Jonson (1638) for having, in his plays, generally avoided vulgar theatrical spectacle: 'Thou laid'st no sieges to the music-room.'

It remains to say a few words about the now generally discarded concept of an Elizabethan 'inner stage'.[14] To many investigators it now seems incredible that such a theory could ever have been generally accepted. Two possible reasons may be suggested for the error. The first is that even so recently as thirty years ago most students of the Elizabethan stage were so exclusively accustomed to illusionistic conventions of the then-contemporary proscenium-arch stage that they could not imagine Elizabethan production without something, however small, that would correspond, however approximately, to the proscenium-arch curtain – after all, Elizabethan stage-directions *do* refer to curtains. A simple answer was the 'inner stage', essentially a small proscenium-arch stage at the back of a so-called outer stage which could be used for the setting of stage-properties out of sight of the audience. The other possible reason for the error is that more than one influential scholar has approached the Elizabethan stage (whether consciously or unconsciously) from the point of view of the Restoration stage. Like its predecessor the playhouse of the Stuart court masque, the Restoration playhouse did have, towards the back of its changeable-scenery stage, an 'alcove' which was used somewhat in the manner advocated by modern apologists for the 'inner stage'; and Restoration plays frequently reflect such an alcove in plot-situations and attendant stage-directions. Thus it seems to have been casually assumed that an Elizabethan discovery was the same thing as a Restoration discovery, hence that the Elizabethan discovery-space was the same thing as the Restoration discovery-space. But neither proposition will withstand scrutiny. The origin of the Elizabethan discovery-space is to be found not in the Renaissance stage of changeable scenery but in the curtained scaffold of the medieval *platea*, whose technique of effecting discoveries was transmitted to the Elizabethan stage, in part perhaps directly, in part perhaps indirectly through the media of the booth stage and the domestic hall screen.[15]

3

THE ACTORS AND STAGING

DANIEL SELTZER

Robert Greene, who had very few kind words for actors, condescended to grant them skills which in his opinion were 'a kind of mechanical labour'. What these skills were, however, he did not tell us; and in this, unfortunately, he was not unlike his contemporaries, even those who admired the actors and wrote graceful tributes to the best of them. An age which took so much greatness for granted took few pains to record in detail the action of the 'mechanics' who embodied dramatic writing on stage. Some description does survive, of course. There are many good-natured allusions, and some not so good-natured, to the ranting voices, bad memories, or thumping stage walks of the hacks, to the flamboyant dress of the profession generally, some enthusiastic eulogies of the excellent actors. The paucity of detailed information about acting *styles* points to the truth of the matter: such observations would hardly have informed Londoners of anything they did not know already. If Thomas Lodge, for example, could speak casually of the 'foul lubber' who '[looked] as pale as the visard of the ghost, which cried so miserably at the theatre, like an oysterwife, "Hamlet revenge"'', we may be reasonably certain that his readers would place the allusion immediately, and that Lodge thought so too. Four centuries later, we should like to know whether that actor playing the Ghost in the lost *Hamlet* before Shakespeare's moved *as* he cried out, how long he held the sound, how high the voice rose in pitch and volume, and where he stood on the stage platform.

Absence of exact documentation of technique may also indicate that the crafts of the Tudor actor, as they had developed, were relatively new ones. That they were not as specifically described as they were generally praised may very likely be due to the fact that there was in the nature of things no time to do so. The drama of the sixteenth and seventeenth centuries in England was an achievement extraordinary not only for its quality, but for the speed with which that quality, in all its varied forms, seems suddenly to have been achieved. In relative terms, its excellence was short-lived, and aspects of it that survived the closing of the theatres and the Restoration were altered considerably by new styles of performance and staging. We have no way of knowing

35

what sort of actor's 'handbook' might have been produced had Parliament not closed the theatres in 1642, but we have only to note that by the end of the eighteenth century, when the craft of acting was as established professionally as the craft of playwriting, there were many detailed accounts of (and by) famous actors in any number of roles. These accounts attest to the truth that theoreticians generally write after the fact; most critical documents about the performing arts – from Aristotle's *Poetics* onwards – show that when a craft such as acting becomes 'established', in the sense that its conventions can be recognized and named, it is then possible to name those practices maintained by some artists, varied by others, or greatly ignored by a few. Even revolutionary artistic achievement can be described in old terms: rules violently broken or happily altered bear still their convenient names. Vasari had no difficulty in describing in detail the new techniques of Michelangelo and Giotto, nor had Berlioz in extensive and specific description of his own practice of orchestration, nor Lewes of the acting methods of Salvini or Kean. But the passage of three or four highly productive decades allowed no time to record the art of the Elizabethan actor, nor to indicate how this art kept pace – as it must have done – with the extraordinarily quick maturation of modes of dramatic writing. Surely the skills of the actors became more complex between, say, 1590 and 1610, and although all available evidence suggests that these skills during the latter part of the period were mainly different in degree and not in kind from those required by earlier repertory, this complexity of technique must have developed too freely and quickly to attempt to codify them, had any Elizabethan or Jacobean been moved to do so.

Surviving eulogies to the great Elizabethan actors consistently praise them for the realism of their characterizations, but this helps us less than it may seem to do. Every age has always maintained that the goal of its representational arts was to mirror nature accurately. As E. H. Gombrich has observed succinctly, 'What we call *seeing* is invariably coloured and shaped by our knowledge (or belief) of what we see,'[1] and for this reason a study of Elizabethan acting methods can help us understand a little more about habits of perception in general in Shakespeare's time. The important question remains, of course, *how* the mirroring of reality was effected, and this problem has elicited a number of opinions. To date, the body of evidence necessary for an accurate estimate has not been collected and published, but the opinions of the opposing camps are easily summarized. A number of critics hold that Elizabethan acting was highly 'formal', that is, that its range of movement, gesture, and vocal expression was more or less categorical, corresponding to a range of rhetorical attitudes capable of being described objectively, and prohibiting (therefore) factors we might wish to call 'inspiration' or 'individual interpretation'. The opposing opinion maintains that much in the style was specifically 'realistic', even 'naturalistic', that certain details of action would have been executed as they might be today, and that there was every reason for a performance by a great actor to exhibit personal inspiration, in every modern sense of the word (indeed, one of the more important eulogies to Burbage seems to document this to some extent). Other critics believe the acting technique was a mixture of rhetorical forms and precise naturalism; and some suggest that this style gradually changed from the early days of the Theatre to those when Shakespeare's plays were being produced at both the Globe and Blackfriars.[2]

The matter cannot be settled here, of course, but after close examination of over two hundred texts, from the earliest interludes through the late Jacobean period, it seems to the present writer that the proponents of a 'mixed' style (or what a modern audience would see as a mixture of various modes) come closest to the truth. But it is of great importance to observe which components of acting styles appear most variable in the mixture, for some practices appear to have been more or less constant throughout the period, while others changed in interesting relationships to altering methods of *writing* plays. It should be observed in passing, however, that those critics who speak of the 'formal' aspects of Elizabethan acting are only commenting upon ways in which it may have appeared different from ours (that dangerous theatrical adjective, 'stylized' – meaning 'mannered' – has come into use only in our own day, and the Elizabethans would not have known what is meant by it). Critics who find evidence for a 'realistic' style, on the other hand, propose simply that much Elizabethan acting looked like ours. Neither mirror image can be entirely correct. That acting at its best was considered 'realistic' there can be no doubt whatever, but there is no more reason to assume that the craft as a whole would resemble ours, than to expect any other form of Renaissance art to resemble its modern equivalent.

Documentation of acting techniques in Elizabethan plays may be divided in three categories. (1) *Printed stage directions* may tell us how something was done on stage, if one excludes those commonly called 'literary' (which may describe, for example, a setting probably not manifest in the playhouse). (2) *'Implicit' stage directions* may be derived from lines in which a character will actually describe what another on stage is doing, or how he is doing it. (3) *Spatial relationships* among actors on stage – that aspect of staging a modern director calls 'blocking', or the 'moves' of an actor – may sometimes be inferred, although great care must be exercised in drawing conclusions.

Possibilities of movement at any given juncture in stage time are of course numerous, but ultimately there are only so many ways an actor, alone or with one or more others, can move – in address (to them or to the audience) or in silence. Most of the time, this evidence is impossible to isolate; but occasionally one spatial relationship, precisely defined, could have taken place only in sequence with another, usually immediately preceding it. Sometimes, if rarely, it is possible in this way to reconstruct two or three such arrangements, and in these cases a tangible picture of stage movement emerges.

From this body of information one may draw conclusions about four aspects of acting style which, taken together, cover everything an actor can do (physically) on stage: (1) *Stage business*, ranging from small details of action relating to the character's own person to facial expressions and movement carried out on lines; (2) *Voice*, primarily in terms of pitch and volume, but including special uses such as parody, and extending as well to such matters as the pacing of speeches, special pauses, tonal quality, and the like; (3) *Stage movement*, in terms of 'blocking', but also considerations such as which areas of the stage were apparently considered 'strongest' and which were utilized for different kinds of action; (4) *Address*, that is, literally the direction of the actor's speech – when he is alone on stage (as when, in a meditative speech, he may as it were address 'himself' only; or, in an explanatory vein, or comic routine, address the audience; or, in a speech of apostrophe, usually in strong emotions, address an imaginary hearer[3]) or with other actors (when he may speak to one or more at a time, or speak without actually addressing any, or in asides to the audience, or alternate among actors, or between them and the audience; also when his speech covers the exit or anticipates the entrance of another actor). Limitations of space naturally prohibit detailed discussion of evidence relating to all of these categories of action. Examples below will indicate the range of actual practice, particularly in terms of stage business and the matter of address. The extent to which they are typical of practice in general, through the period, will be indicated by summary reference to texts from which individual quotation is impractical.

In *2 The Return from Parnassus*, Kemp is made to criticize bad academic actors who 'never speak in their walk, but at the end of the stage, just as though in walking with a fellow we should never speak but at a stile, a gate, or a ditch, where a man can go no further'. The observation is good evidence that this component of a technique we should regard as 'natural' was common practice. Detailed 'small' business not necessarily relating to the subject matter of lines simultaneously spoken, however, must be considered a category of stage business distinct from action which might – in a more 'formal' mode –

demonstrate an internalized emotion or motivation. Let us examine the former category first.

There is enough evidence in plays from the earlier decades of the period to prove such business no innovation. On an average, in plays with dates of composition falling between 1560 and 1589, there is definite evidence that this convention took place during 4 per cent of the total lines in any given text. Roughly the same percentage applies to plays written between 1590 and 1608, and from 1609 until the closing of the theatres there is evidence that 'small' stage business existed on 6 per cent of the total lines in a play.[4] The convention may be said, therefore, to have been a fairly consistent one throughout the period; the small increase in its frequency during the last three decades under consideration is really not significant. At its most sophisticated, the practice does seem remarkably similar to a modern manner of action. Consider Palamon and Arcite as they talk while involved in the highly detailed business of adjusting each other's armour. One cannot escape the impression of great flexibility and natural pace of delivery:

> ARC. ...Do I pinch you?
> PAL.   No.
> ARC. Is't not too heavy?
> PAL.   I have worn a lighter,
> But I shall make it serve.
> ARC.   I'll buckle it close.
> PAL. By any means.
> ARC. You care not for a grand-guard?
> PAL. No, no! we'll use no horses. I perceive
> You would be fain at that fight.
> ARC.   I am indifferent.
> PAL. Faith, so am I. Good cousin, thrust the buckle
> Through far enough.
> ARC.   I warrant you.

Shortly after this exchange, they recall battles of earlier days.

> ARC.   When I saw you charge first,
> Methought I heard a dreadful clap of thunder
> Break from the troop.
> PAL.   But still before that flew
> The lightning of your valour. Stay a little.
> Is not this piece too strait?
>   (*The Two Noble Kinsmen* III, vi, 54–62, 82–6)

Not many years earlier, an episode in *Antony and Cleopatra* would have required almost identical business and use of properties, and implies the same ease and natural pacing (apparently as attainable on the stage of the Globe as that of Blackfriars):

> ANT.   . . . Come.
> CLEO.   Nay, I'll help too.
>   What's this for?
> ANT.   Ah, let be, let be! Thou art
>   The armourer of my heart. False, false; this, this.
> CLEO. Sooth, la, I'll help. Thus it must be.
> ANT.   Well, well;
>   We shall thrive now. . . .
> CLEO. Is not this buckled well?
> ANT.   Rarely, rarely!
>
> (IV, iv, 4–11)

Examples from the earlier plays of Shakespeare are of course frequent; Troilus's removal of his armour in his first dialogue with Pandarus would have been accomplished with the same ease with which Hotspur dons his while talking with Lady Percy – and the assumption of various disguises in the comedies provides further parallels.

Evidence is plentiful in plays by Shakespeare's early contemporaries, including those by Marlowe, where stage 'pictures' were perhaps not so static as has often been assumed; Tamburlaine dresses in his captured armour while speaking to Zenocrate (237–47, 250), and in Part Two, Calyphas and his servant play cards while conversing (3740–6) and the hero, in a cumulative description of his victories, uses a map as he speaks (4519–51); and in Faustus's great opening speech, there is no question that the property books – Aristotle, Galen, Justinian, Jerome's Bible, and, finally, those of necromancy – provided opportunity for this category of business on specific lines (33, 40, 55, 66, 77–8) – just as Barabas's money bags and jewels would have been used in the comparable scene of *The Jew of Malta*. The important point about all of these examples is that whether the business simply punctuates and makes vivid the subject matter of the lines, or whether it represents an effort (by playwright or actor) to add realistic details to the stage world of the character (e.g. '*Enter Master Frankford, as it were brushing the crumbs from his clothes with a napkin, as newly risen from supper*' (*A Woman Killed With Kindness*, S.D. at III, ii, 26)), the Elizabethan actors obviously had easy access to an enlargement of a stage personality's realistic world, and that throughout the period that access was absolutely conventional. Indeed, Nashe's complaint about actors not occupied in a crucial action or speech who, too often, 'stroke [their] beards to make action, [and] play with [their] codpiece points',[5] a complaint echoed later by Hamlet, suggests that the bad habits of some actors have remained the same for four centuries.

The second category of stage business – that which to some extent would externalize a psychologically oriented feeling or motivation, actually *demonstrating* to an audience the inner life of a character – is in some ways more interesting than evidence of 'small' business, for it pertains directly to questions of our own staging of the plays. This category of evidence is most revealing of Elizabethan projection of psychology, and is therefore relevant to our own inquiries into such matters as an actor's 'identification' with his stage character. Once again let us begin with a scene representing acting methods late in the period. In *Henry VIII*, a scene with Wolsey and certain nobles, and afterwards the King, provides a complete book of directions for action intended to convey deep emotional turmoil, and indicates precisely a series of gestures which are most suggestive in any consideration of the over-all style of acting. Norfolk, Suffolk, Surrey, and the Lord Chamberlain have been discussing events relative to the King's divorce, when Wolsey and Cromwell enter. Immediately, Norfolk says of the Cardinal, 'Observe, observe, he's moody' (III, ii, 75); nothing has been said, but Norfolk – and the audience – have seen the Cardinal frowning (cf. S.D., III, ii, 203; v, i. 87–8; S.D., v, iii, 113). Wolsey, not observing the others on stage, speaks of the letters Henry has opened, and, dismissing Cromwell, informs the audience of his plans and fears (85–90). The lords who watch have not, of course, 'heard' Wolsey, but Norfolk observes, 'He's discontented' (91). After the others comment, the Cardinal resumes his meditation about Anne Bullen and his fears of Cranmer (94–103). For the third time Norfolk comments on Wolsey's state of mind: 'He is vex'd at something' (103). Here the King enters, reading (as he moves into the acting area) the inventory of Wolsey's possessions, and, not noticing the Cardinal (which suggests that Wolsey has moved to one corner of the stage – probably diagonally opposite whichever door used by Henry for his entrance), asks for him. Norfolk replies:

> My lord, we have
> Stood here observing him. Some strange commotion
> Is in his brain: he bites his lip and starts,
> Stops on a sudden, looks upon the ground,
> Then lays his finger on his temple; straight
> Springs out into fast gait; then stops again,
> Strikes his breast hard; and anon he casts
> His eye against the moon. In most strange postures
> We have seen him set himself.
> (111–19)

Norfolk's catalogue must be accurate, of course; the audience has also seen what the actor did who played Wolsey, and even if Shakespeare

41

is anxious to emphasize the Cardinal's feelings, any added observation in Norfolk's speech would have been built upon the action just ended. Wolsey's business was evidently categorical action for great inner perturbation – 'There is a mutiny in's mind,' Henry says. Biting the lip had long been a standard piece of business (e.g. Catesby, *Richard III*, IV, ii, 27: 'The King is angry; see, he gnaws his lip'; Desdemona, *Othello*, V, ii, 46: 'Alas, why gnaw you so your nether lip?'). In addition we have sudden movement into a fast walk, and sudden stops, quick alternation of looks upward and downward, pressing the finger against the temple, and striking the breast. It would be possible, in fact, following Norfolk's summary, to insert stage-directions for the lines of Wolsey's speech; in any case, the acting style clearly involved more than a few gestures (for a relatively short semi-soliloquy) and apparently eschewed small or over-subtle facial expression. It demanded considerable movement across the stage. It was, to say the least, a 'large' style, and *Henry VIII* is a late play.

At least so far as the evidence suggests, certain emotions did not demand increasingly nuanced stage expression as the years passed. A range of attitudes and gestures very similar to Wolsey's were very likely used by Burbage in early performances of *Othello*. The violence with which Othello's jealousy would have been expressed is unquestionable; it fits too well into an emblematic description – identical to many contemporary analyses of love maladies – to suggest anything less than conventional histrionic treatment. The angry questions Othello puts to Desdemona at the end of III, iv provoke Emilia's question, 'Is not this man jealous?' They have been stock questions, and would have been accompanied by similarly categorical gestures and looks. Generally, Othello's role at this point falls into the type called 'hasty', in the Prologue to a manuscript play, *The Cyprian Conqueror*, requiring 'fuming, and scratching the head, etc.'[6] But there is a more detailed source book for description of the violently jealous hero. After noting that 'your bravest soldiers and most generous spirits are [most readily] enervated with [the passions of Heroical Love] when they surrender to feminine blandishments' (*The Anatomy of Melancholy*, III, 2, 1, 1), Burton goes on to describe the effects of such passions when they become corrupted by jealousy; and it is a very theatrical description:

Besides those strange gestures of staring, frowning, grinning, rolling of eyes, menacing, ghastly looks, broken pace, interrupt, precipitate, half-turns... [he] will sometimes sigh, weep, sob for anger, swear and belie, slander any man, curse, threaten...and then, eftsoons, impatient as he is, rave, roar, and lay about him like a mad man, thump her sides, drag her about perchance... his eye is never off hers; he gloats...on her, accurately observing on whom she looks, who looks at her, what she saith, doth, at dinner, at supper, sitting, walking, at home, abroad...affrighted with every small object; why did she smile, why did she pity him, commend him?...a whore, an arrant whore!

(III, 3, 2)

Desdemona observes her husband's 'fatal' rolling of his eyes (v, ii, 37–8); he weeps, his looks reflect 'a bloody passion', he strikes her, flatters her sarcastically; in short, his action seems to run parallel to Burton's catalogue. It is also very suggestive of the details included in Norfolk's speech about Wolsey. The emotional pressures upon the two men are of course quite different, and yet the evidence in this instance points with some certainty to the fact that the actors who played these characters must have utilized components of physicalization and movement that were all but identical.

Demonstrative business and moves were not always required, of course, to express depth of feeling. Plays from the later years of the period contain many examples of what a modern actor would call business suggestive of 'internalized' emotion, an intensity *felt* by the actor 'in' character. One example must stand for hundreds. At a particularly lovely moment towards the end of *Pericles*, the hero, not yet realizing that his daughter stands before him, pushes Marina from him. He reviews certain phrases she has spoken, and asks her to repeat them. 'I said, my lord, if you did know my parentage, / You would not do me violence,' she replies (v, i. 100–1). 'I do think so,' he says; 'Pray you turn your eyes upon me.' Now Marina has had an aside a few lines previous ('I will desist; / But there is something glows upon my cheek, / And whispers in mine ear "Go not till he speak"' (95–7)) – and it is possible that the actor was to turn away from Pericles on this; but it is clear in any case that Marina was to speak her next lines still turned from him – which would be the way a modern actress would want to render them.

Plays from the earlier years also reveal a surprising mixture of 'demonstrative' and 'internalized' emotion, as far as may be inferred from stage business. In the old play of *King Leir* (1588–94), a Messenger delivers to Ragan letters from Gonerill; she opens one (1169), and is actually given two lines to cover – in our terms, quite realistically – this detail of business: 'How fares our royal sister? / I did leave her, at my parting, in good health' (1170–71). At this point a stage-direction reads, *She reads the letter, frowns and stamps* (1172), and the Messenger's speech which follows describes her action just as Norfolk's describes Wolsey's:

> See how her colour comes and goes again,
> Now red as scarlet, now as pale as ash:

43

See how she knits her brow, and bites her lips,
And stamps, and makes a dumb shew of disdain,
Mixed with revenge, and violent extremes.

(1173–7)

The first two lines of this speech are of course 'literary' directions, evoking a reaction no actor, of any period (no matter how skilled in any 'Method'), could effect at will (cf. Brutus' observation to Cassius that an 'angry spot doth glow on Caesar's brow'); the others no doubt tell us exactly what happened. Whatever the relative quality of the writing in each case, the *style* seems hardly more 'primitive' than that documented for Wolsey's action some twenty-three years later.

Moreover, in many texts from quite early in the period under discussion, evidence may be found for internalized emotion – or at least an effort on the playwright's part to achieve it – comparable to many moments in plays written after 1600. A most interesting combination of modes occurs in Marlowe's *Edward II*, whatever its exact date a reasonably early play. Queen Isabel stands silent while her husband's escape and bad fortune are discussed (1831–9, 1841–50), until Sir John of Hainault addresses her, having noticed something about her stance or mood (as rendered by the actor playing her): 'Madam, what resteth, why stand ye in a muse?' (1851). The attitude of a 'muse' (frequently described in the texts as 'a brown study' or 'trance') was very common indeed throughout the period – there are some eighty references to it, in many different dramatic situations, in the plays used for this study. What action it involved is difficult to infer; but at this point in *Edward II* there can be no question that the Queen's silence and her mood, however acted, were meant to convey an *internalized* response. As would be the case in modern production technique, the convention required, apparently, minimal physicalization, or demonstration. Yet earlier in the play, after Isabel's lament on her estrangement from Edward (466–82), various nobles enter, among them Lancaster, who observes, 'Look where the sister of the king of France, / Sits wringing of her hands, and beats her breast' (483–4).

Evidently variations of intensity did not signal categorical forms of stage business, for playwrights frequently intended the actor to reveal in some way that his emotions were too deep not only for words, but for large action indicating those emotions. The 'muse' was a common device for such an effort, but there were others, even in a text as early and as relatively unsophisticated as Pickeryng's *Horestes* (1567). Here Horestes, about to order the execution of his mother, and in conflict of motivation, is directed to '[sigh] hard', although he is given no words to speak; the Vice watches him and observes, 'Jesu God, how still he sits...' (S.D., 891–3; 893). Such deep sighs seem also to have been common practice throughout the period; there are more than sixty examples of them in the plays considered, all of them similar in intention to that 'so piteous and profound', which Ophelia reports that Hamlet 'rais'd', revealing an inner state so intense 'As it did seem to shatter all his bulk'. One cannot escape the impression, in reviewing all of these examples of demonstrated emotion, that Elizabethan practice, while immensely diversified, invariably provided physicalization of some kind, however it might vary in scope, to represent inner feelings – one might almost say, to *describe* them. Pickeryng's effort to deepen our impression of his hero may seem to us shallow and clichéd, but it is really the same in kind as Peele's Edward I, who listens quietly to Eleanor's death-bed confession of her adultery with Edmund – and, *as she speaks*, is directed to turn and [*behold*] *his brother wofully* (2755): a move and an expression that would seem to us 'modern' and full of nuance.

But one must be cautious. Edward's turn and look, Isabel's 'muse', Horestes' sigh, and Marina's aside with its accompanying move all suggest a habit of mirroring reality in fact no more 'internalized' or psychologically oriented in our sense, than were the larger gestures, lip-biting, rapid walks, and breast-thumping of Ragan, Othello, and Wolsey. In the true sense of the word, they were 'representational' artifice; the modern actor would call them 'presentational'. Even the least physicalized of them indicate an acting style which we would consider, if it were unqualified by other components of the art, 'formal' and 'large'. More, this aspect of the over-all style does not seem to have altered as the years passed. In Munday's *John-a-Kent and John-a-Cumber* (c. 1589), certain characters are confused as to the exact location of the invisible Shrimp's voice (1118–24; S.D., 1123–4), and in *Arden of Feversham* (c. 1591) a whole scene must be played as though the characters are moving through fog (1721–98); the stage directions and lines suggest a style neither more nor less 'large' than that used twenty-two or twenty-three years later by the 'charm'd' captives of Prospero, their 'understanding' having been made 'foul and muddy' (*Tempest*, S.D. at v, i, 57; 58 ff.), and their action commensurately demonstrative of their inner state.

The collection of evidence above pertains to acted 'business', and suggests little change of practice over forty or fifty years – years that witnessed a remarkable development in the dramatist's craft. It is important to have a detailed, if summarized, view of stage business, because it is here that one achieves the clearest over-all view of a mixed stylistic practice. But it is in the matter of address that the gradual *change* of style assumed by some critics can be detected. The flexibility with which an actor alters direction of his address implies many other characteristics of his style – for example, a corresponding flexibility of stage movement, individual stance, and blocking of stage 'pictures'. Flexibility of address, however, depends in turn on a more basic element of theatre: the ways in which the texts themselves may or may not require it. The development of acting style during the Elizabethan and Jacobean periods of drama may be said to depend most upon the extraordinary development of the techniques of dialogue by the major playwrights – particularly Shakespeare, Webster, Jonson, Middleton, and Ford. Of secondary importance, though of great interest, is the steadily decreasing emphasis, by these playwrights and others, on the device of soliloquy. Speaking in the most general terms, an examination of the texts dating from 1608 on reveals an increase in the number of 'ensemble' episodes accompanying the decline of soliloquy techniques; and, as has always been the case among professional actors of talent and practicality, crafts of the stage metamorphosed precisely along the lines implicit in the playwrights' dramaturgy. (A comparable phenomenon took place when Stanislavsky transformed the acting styles of the Moscow Art Theatre to answer the immensely complex requirements of Chekhov's new scripts.) When the average number of players on stage in any given episode is only *two* – the average in texts dating earlier than 1585 – the possibilities for flexible alteration of address are of course minimal; similarly, during the earlier period, solo address – whether in an 'apostrophic' or meditative mode, or delivered to the audience – did not require the remarkable nuance of stage practice typical of the later drama. One can locate in the earlier plays long sections of solo speech and dialogue containing many modulations of address, but the consistency with which the texts of later years reveal such modulation is remarkable.

One of the more common forms of such modulation is that alteration which takes place when a character speaks to another who is leaving the acting area (usually covering the exit, and, in fact, sometimes enabling us to know the exact line on which the second actor leaves the individual or group), or sees the entrance of another and comments on it, covering in a similar way the new actor's approach to the acting area. This form of address can be delivered just as easily, of course, by the exiting or entering actor; frequently it would involve address over the shoulder, or coming to a short stop in the exit walk, which would then be resumed after the line or lines. In the earlier period – up to, say, 1580 – this form of delivery covered, when it occurred, on an average, six lines. Usually these lines involved some descriptive comment on the approaching (or departing) character, delivered either to another person already on stage or, in many cases, to the audience. The average number of lines used in such 'anticipatory' or 'covering' address in the period up to 1605–6 is closer to three lines for each occurrence; and – although mathematical exactness is probably not only impossible but subject to varying line readings by each student of the subject – the average seems to drop off still more in plays written between 1606 and the closing of the theatres. The use of the convention itself seems to decrease; in Shakespeare's *Pericles, Cymbeline, The Winter's Tale, The Tempest,* and *Henry VIII,* and in Shakespeare's and Fletcher's *The Two Noble Kinsmen,* the average number of lines used in this category of address is only two – and such address occurs infrequently. In earlier plays, the use of such address was twofold; mainly it served the practical purpose of covering stage-time while a character left or approached the acting area, but occasionally, and more important, it served an expository or narrative purpose. It would lead almost always into solo speech by the actor still on stage, for the joining of episode to episode in most early plays of the period was accomplished purely in terms of explanatory soliloquy. In this sort of speech, action – and thought – would be *described*, and not acted out, or truly 'thought'. But even as the device of the soliloquy became increasingly sophisticated, the convention itself became less and less necessary. If the average of persons on stage, during each episode of a play in the early period, was only two, the average per episode after 1605 is five.[7] Although short asides (averaging, usually, no more than five lines) remain a frequent practice in later years, most of the lines in such scenes require, in one mode or another, flexible alteration of address among the characters present. (This, in turn, would have had an obvious effect on stage movement and positioning.)

Adequate discussion of the techniques of soliloquy would require many pages, and one can only summarize here the development, and subsequent decline, that influenced an over-all acting style. The convention was old even in the early days of Tudor drama, and many critics have observed the range of materials which could be included in such speech. From the early interludes onwards examples of purely introspective or explanatory soliloquies are plentiful; and there are many speeches which one might call 'apostrophic'. Frequently, these modes of address blended. Students of the subject have always wanted to know how often this sort of speech was in fact delivered to the spectators, but the general opinion that such direct address took place very often has never been adequately documented. In the solo speeches of the early 'Vice' characters, the actor would sometimes actually pick out a member of the audience for specific address, referring again and again to 'you' – although equally often this would imply a collective object of his plot descriptions. One suspects that other forms of the soliloquy – a hero's meditations or laments, for example – were also addressed at times to the spectators; but this is harder to prove, especially as dramatic writing gave the characters inner personalities in terms of action instead of purely external description (whether by others or themselves). Nevertheless, there is good evidence of some audience address in introspective speeches from early plays; the writing is unpolished, the machinery creaks, but the manner of the actor is in some cases much clearer. And one may assume that the convention was not entirely dropped with increased subtlety of writing.

In Garter's *Susanna* (*c.* 1568), for example, Joachim comments on the lack of moral government, partly in meditation as he glances about the stage for the judges, but partly in audience address as he prays for blessings upon each spectator as well as for himself (836–51). That part of the speech which is clearly set in direct address is mainly a device to help the actor get off-stage, but even without it, and the explanatory tone in the beginning, one could observe that the sententious tone of the lines rings of explanation to a group of hearers. In an earlier play, *Calisto and Melebea* (*c.* 1527), Calisto prays for Sempronio's good fortune, then says,

> To pass the time now will I walk
> Up and down within mine orchard,
> And to myself go [commune] and talk,
> And pray that fortune to me be not hard,
> Longing to hear whether made or marred;
> My message shall return by my servant Sempronio;
> Thus, farewell my lordis, for a while I will go.

> (306–12)

The tone here is not sententious but personal. The character *presents*, in fact, the subject matter for a soliloquy which the playwright did not wish – or did not know how – to compose. Although the speech is, in its own terms, 'introspective', it rings of explanation, and it may be said that Calisto *announces* what his emotions are, but does not actually express them. They are presented much as Joachim, in *Susanna*, presents *sententiae* upon moral government.

These examples have been chosen arbitrarily, but even though they come from the very early period they indicate roughly certain conventional practices. In many cases, speeches which one might ordinarily categorize as addressed to an 'imaginative rather than actual, mute rather than responsive' auditory,[8] actually contain some evidence that at least part of the lines were oriented toward the audience. Speeches from *Clyomon and Clamydes*, from *Cambises*, *Horestes*, and *Appius and*

Virginia, from plays performed in schools, in the University halls, at court, and upon public stages, suggest direct address in all types of soliloquies – usually with the Vice's common intention of explanation, but more and more often in purely introspective, meditative speech. Indeed there is every reason to assume a certain amount of direct address *whenever* a character was alone on stage, that it frequently took place in the execution of asides, and that there is no evidence for less use of the convention in the great plays of Shakespeare, whenever soliloquy might occur. Indeed, Joachim's observations on the insolence of office require direct address neither more nor less than Hamlet's do; and Poverty's walk about the platform, and his speech to the audience as he moved (*Impatient Poverty* (c. 1547), 994–5 ff.), may be the mould not only for all the prodigal sons of the Tudor interludes, hawking their wares as Mater and Pater occupy another part of the stage, but also for such soliloquies as Ferdinand's, as he bears Prospero's logs, while the magician and the princess stand nearby. It is well to remember John Russell Brown's observation that any sort of direct speech in this drama was not addressed to the audience 'as if it were in another world'[9] – but that a sense of reality in these plays moved in both directions across the edge of the platform. Since an actor will usually project speech to a listener as though some sort of response were possible, and even forthcoming, we may perhaps conclude that audience address in the plays of this period placed the spectator in a truly creative relationship with the actor. This relationship existed not only during solo speech on stage, but also would have been reinforced as actors directed asides to the audience during ensemble scenes. Thus the total action of the play would be punctuated at frequent intervals with speech literally including the audience in narrative action or introspective thought.

In the early period of Tudor drama, a conservative estimate indicates that about 8 per cent of each play was addressed either entirely to the audience, or contained speeches beginning with audience address which were then directed back to a stage area. This estimate is based upon a figure of 1,900 lines, on the average, in each play, with some manner of solo speech in which direct address occurred taking place (again on the average) five times in the course of each play, each speech averaging about thirty lines. This set of figures does not change much as one moves into the greater period of the drama, although of course certain texts, considered individually, range far from the norm. Nor is there any evidence, as the years pass, that direct address was associated more or less with solo speech than it had been in the earlier period. What does take place, as I have suggested, is that the frequency of the convention of soliloquy itself diminishes dramatically. When it occurs, even in the late plays of Shakespeare, and the later plays of his contemporaries, it is usually possible to recognize the category of solo speech that is in each case the archetype – almost always recalling a form used in the very early years of the period; but it occurs much less often.

Nor does the less frequent appearance of the device coincide with the availability, to Shakespeare's company or others, of private theatres. Although Shakespeare's art in the composition of soliloquies reached its height during the period 1600–6, when the major tragedies were written, there was already some indication that *certain kinds of action did not require the convention as often.* Except perhaps for Angelo's rather short *tour de force,* we do not remember *Measure for Measure, Troilus and Cressida,* or *All's Well That Ends Well* for their soliloquies; in *Troilus and Cressida,* in fact, there are no speeches of great importance which really qualify to be so called. In *Othello,* Shakespeare maintained and polished the oldest of the old categories of solo speech – that of the Vice – in distributing Iago's brilliant soliloquies of explanation and anticipation (many of them couched quite explicitly in a form of direct address; e.g. 'And what's he, then, that says I play the villain...?'), but the hero really has only one speech which may be called a soliloquy (iii, iii, 262–81). There may be much audience address in *King Lear* which takes the form of asides or short speeches that bridge episodes of action, and a large part of i, ii is given over to Edmund's solo speeches, one apostrophic (1–22) and one a prose speech of character 'explanation' (111–27). Considering the text as a whole, however, there is little use of the device. *Macbeth* and *Hamlet* are different matters, of course, for the action of the play moves in direct proportion to the development (or disintegration) of the hero's mind. In both plays, about 10 per cent of stage time is consumed by the solo lines of each hero. In *Antony and Cleopatra,* the way in which the device is used in the last plays of Shakespeare, and in many of his contemporaries writing after 1610, begins to take shape. The play has only one big set-piece – Enobarbus' lament on his desertion – but such meditative moments as Antony's 'I must from this enchanting queen break off' pass quickly into another sort of action; this, for example, is embedded in a nine-line speech on the death of Fulvia – subject matter which, in an earlier play, might have suggested to the playwright a full-blown soliloquy. An examination of *Pericles, Cymbeline, The Winter's Tale, The Tempest, Henry VIII,* and *The Two Noble Kinsmen* reveals on the whole a further diminishing of emphasis upon soliloquy. Counting all speeches spoken by a character alone on stage – including Prologues, Epilogues, and Gower's choruses – and by characters in asides longer than five lines each, there are in *Pericles* 389 lines of solo speech, 401 in *Cymbeline*, 146 in *The Winter's Tale*, 87 in *The Tempest*, 69 in *Henry VIII*, and – a wholesome warning against quick judgements! – 210 in *The Two Noble Kinsmen*. For what the observation is worth, there are only 14 lines of solo speech, aside from Gower's, in the last three acts of *Pericles* (the acts generally agreed to be Shakespeare's); the relatively few lines of solo speech in *Henry VIII* occur as often in the so-called 'Shakespearian' scenes as in the 'Fletcherian'. The question of authorship in *The Two Noble Kinsmen* is too complicated to make many distinctions; but whichever playwright is responsible for the mad scenes of the Gaoler's daughter is responsible for the sudden alteration in the pattern.

One must not underestimate the theatrical effect of this gradual change in the later plays of the period. It occurs, in plays by Shakespeare's contemporaries, in roughly the same proportion as in the last romances, and it is an alteration in the very texture of stage artifice, in the means used by dramatists to advance action. The actual response of the spectators, taken in sum, would be altered commensurately, for a special habit of response was rendered less and less central to the actor's projection of plays with fewer soliloquies, each of them, therefore, containing less direct address – and *more* modulation within scenes of ensemble and dialogue. In the last plays of Shakespeare, there remain of course several soliloquies, some of them truly in the old style (e.g. Posthumus', on women, *Cymbeline* II, v, 1–35), and many half-soliloquies, usually spoken with reference to others actually on stage (e.g. Leontes' in the second episode of *The Winter's Tale*). But considered as a whole one's impression of these plays as theatrical pieces has a distinctly new emphasis.

This emphasis corresponds to the critical opinion, widely held, that the last Shakespearian plays have 'lost' a focus and concentration typical of the major tragedies, and that this concentration is replaced by other dramaturgical factors. At least part of the focus in the major tragedies was achieved, speaking for a moment purely in stage terms, through the skilful use of soliloquy. This device aided in gradual concentration inward upon the mind of the hero, always shown to strive painfully towards understanding, always true to the agony of a vision limited by mortality. The hero's *self*-exposition at regular points in the course of the play, especially true of Hamlet and Macbeth, actually effects one element of action, and simultaneously the acting methods required to embody it. In later plays – and not only those by Shakespeare – the dramaturgy concerns itself with a fabric of action at once shallower and more complex: shallower in point of 'character', since the sequence of cause and event is now more important than internalized motivation; and more complex in plot-line, which must spread more widely, with greater speed, involving as it does so many more characters. And of these characters it is often more important to know where they are geographically, and where they are about to go, than to know at length what they are thinking. Shakespeare's development – beginning perhaps most noticeably with *King Lear* and *Antony and Cleopatra* – had been towards a more generalized vision, a fabric in which the total effect would be more important than the probing in depth of an individual mind. He began to practise, then, as to a lesser extent did many of his contemporaries, ways to compress the rhythms of human speech so that much of the elongation implicit in the device of soliloquy was now not only unnecessary, but would have changed his new characters into the sort of personalities destructive to the dramaturgy of romance.

Leontes' soliloquy (*The Winter's Tale* I, ii, 109–46) is the best example of the developed form late in the period. Really a half-soliloquy, it is spoken with other actors on stage – and in part to one of them, the boy, Mamillius. In its physicalization it would perhaps not have varied greatly from many others, earlier in the period; but vocally and in terms of the actor's stance, corresponding to extraordinary requirements of modulated address, it is entirely different. In its first part, it requires modulation from attention to the scene across the stage area to a stance of meditation, then to the child standing nearby. As the speech progresses, its tempo and stress change suddenly, and the rhythm and diction mirror the chaos of Leontes' mind, much as the tortured syntax, paralleling the disjointed sequence of thought, becomes an implicit stage direction for Hamlet, in his first soliloquy. But the process in the *Hamlet* soliloquy is one of self-interruption, the subject matter moving from the specific to the general and back again. To render it adequately required – as is true today – an ability to modulate tone and tempo within the individual line; nevertheless there is a regularity about it that is missing from Leontes' speech. Here there is a swifter alteration of specific address, with interruption representative not simply of a change of subject, but of *degree* in the character's very ability to articulate it. When this articulation is meant to be more difficult, the diction itself becomes more abstract; and to render this theatrically, implying the concentration of idea in the character's mind, must have required – as, again, it does today – an entirely new approach on the part of the actor.

It will be seen, in summary, that certain aspects of Elizabethan acting style remained more or less the same throughout the decades of greatest production. Always there had been conventional ways to enlarge the detailed reality of a stage personality's physical world, by means of 'small' stage business carried forward on lines; and always there seem to have been recognizably categorical practices for 'demonstrating' various levels of inward emotional states – some of them, in our terms, 'large', and some amazingly modern in their minimal physical manifestations. An over-all impression, however, conveys a sense of style we should probably call 'formalized'. On the other hand, the details of address – absolutely organic to details of play-*writing* – must have metamorphosed very greatly between, say, 1580 and 1595; and as dramaturgical fashions and preferences changed after that year, such details continued to alter accordingly. The skills of the players had to keep up with the requirements of their scripts, and the phenomenon of their training – about which we know next to nothing – must have been truly extraordinary. The actor chosen to play Cambises, for example, must have been an excellent artist, in terms of the repertory companies then at work; but one wonders if the young Marlowe would have attempted *Tamburlaine* had there been no Alleyn to render the totally new requirements of that script! But the development of which I have spoken may be seen, perhaps, most clearly if one wonders how actors trained as Alleyn may have been could approach the new vocal techniques implicit in such roles as Ferdinand, in *The Duchess of Malfi*, or Prospero. We have said little about characters in plays written for the boys' companies; but it is fascinating that the evidence collected for this study comes as frequently, in the later years of the period, from the children's texts as from the public repertory – and hardly ever does it present new or categorically different documentation of acting style. The devices of theatrical style inevitably change from year to year, but stage abilities and physical development of adolescent and pre-adolescent boys do not – and this leads one to assume, if only as a general conclusion, that the remarkable nuance of address (for example) that is implicit in the late plays of Shakespeare or Fletcher, and which requires for adequate presentation now not only an actor of talent but a man of experience and even wisdom, was beyond the children's abilities: *if* we also assume that such nuance would have been rendered as we think it should be today. The truth of the matter is that the very tonality, pace, and general characterization of a children's production in the Jacobean period can never be grasped through any evidence available to us, and is one aspect of Renaissance acting in England lost in the flux of time.

Of the actors themselves – Greene's 'mechanics' – it must be said that they must have been unlike most actors at work today. If in nothing else, they were remarkable for the spectrum of their perceptions and physical abilities, for even if they failed frequently (as they must have done) their successes were responsible for the survival of the theatre's most valuable possessions. Their memories must have been phenomenal and their stamina – physically and vocally – unlike any-thing required of repertory actors, anywhere, today. Whatever the categorical devices may have been that helped them learn the action that suited their roles, they obviously achieved – to the satisfaction of the most demanding Elizabethan spectators – a truth to life that graced their scripts just as greatly as the achievement of those scripts ennobled and dignified them.

4

SHAKESPEARE'S READING

G. K. HUNTER

An inquiry into 'Shakespeare's reading' is difficult to confine within manageable bounds unless, of course, it is stopped short of any interpretation and confined to book titles, quotations, and a list of the stories that Shakespeare is presumed to have used. And even in such a truncated form the inquiry is bedevilled by the problem of what constitutes evidence. The game of literary parallels is one that can be played with dashing but irrelevant freedom. As will be suggested later, the wisdom of the Elizabethans was nearly all traditional wisdom; the point in the tradition that the modern critic selects as a 'source' is often arbitrary and tendentious. Such publications as M. P. Tilley's *Dictionary of the Proverbs in England in the Sixteenth and Seventeenth Centuries* (1950) may help to curb the wilder excesses of the past; but the ambition to discover new things must continue to operate, and no doubt will continue to metamorphose the similar into the identical.

On the other side of the subject lies the opposite danger: of finding oneself claiming to describe Shakespeare's mind – a task that might seem best left to clairvoyants. And yet the reading habits of any man are an important aspect of his mental habits. Shakespeare's mind was certainly no mere waiting-room in which quotations marked time between one book and another. The evidences of his reading are fragmentary and discontinuous; it is obvious that he absorbed and modified whatever he read. It may be dangerously facile to apply straight to Shakespeare the evidence about Coleridge's creative reading that Professor Livingston Lowes assembled in *The Road to Xanadu* – for Shakespeare was not a nineteenth-century poet but an Elizabethan playwright – but Lowes's image of the hooks and eyes of Coleridge's imagination may provide the best picture of Shakespeare's mental processes that is available to us. And that such a process was involved somewhere in Shakespeare's creative mind seems to be proved by the recurrent associative patterns discussed by Walter Whiter and by E. A. Armstrong.

ELIZABETHAN READING HABITS

The Coleridgean image of Shakespeare's reading has the disadvantage that it seems to isolate Shakespeare from many of his contemporaries. There may be some advantage therefore in taking a brief preliminary glance at Elizabethan reading habits in general, to suggest the background of expectations about reading against which Shakespeare lived his professional life.

Reading was one of the skills to which the Humanists, like other educators, devoted a great deal of energy. They were, of course, largely concerned with the new materials for reading – Greco-Roman literature – but the question 'How should we read these books?' was an integral one which had to be faced and answered. And it was answered in a surprisingly medieval way. The medieval imitation of the classics, writes Karl Burdach (quoted by Roberto Weiss), 'proceeds according to the method of the glossator, that is to say it takes details, choice and beautiful sentences, with a collector's precision; it is a matter of indifference to the collector where they came from'. In the Elizabethan period the names of the classical authors had become important, but it was a long time before the spirit of the work from which quotations came controlled the use of the quotations.

The obvious and standard method of using one's reading to collect information and details of rhetorical structure (and in consequence, the educators hoped, a classical style of life) was by way of a commonplace book. This was a collection of wise sayings, similes and other materials, under moral headings: 'Abstinence', 'Adversity', 'Affection', 'Ambition' etc. And here, as in so many other fields, it seems as if the method of the schools dominated the whole cultural scene. We find Sir Philip Sidney urging his brother Robert to keep up his collections:

And so as in a table, be it a witty word, of which Tacitus is full, sentences, as of which Livy, or of similitudes, whereof Plutarch, straight to lay it up in the right place of his storehouse.

As late as 1720 Swift feels it necessary to dissuade a 'young gentleman lately entered into holy orders' from relying on his commonplace book, lest he produce 'a manifest incoherent piece of patchwork'. This points to the obvious danger. Much Elizabethan writing is, in fact, related to reading as patchwork is to rags; but that patchworks or (less pejoratively) mosaics need not be manifestly incoherent may be suggested by Jonson's *Sejanus* and Webster's *The Duchess of Malfi* – works largely made up of quotations.

The copiousness of the Elizabethan style was often capable of absorbing within an exuberant unity the multitude of quotations it contained. The danger that Swift points to seemed unimportant. Indeed there was a constant demand for further aids to *copia*. A steady stream of epitomes and digests, anthologies, nosegays, gardens of wisdom and wellsprings of witty conceits flowed from the press. These, already digested and broken down under topics, saved one the labour of making one's own commonplace book. Under certain circumstances they might save altogether the labour of consecutive reading.

SHAKESPEARE AND THE CLASSICS

The extensive use of books of quotations has an obvious bearing on the long-debated question of Shakespeare's classical attainments. This was an age which loved the panache of classical display more than the understanding of authors. Sir Jack Daw in Jonson's *Epicoene* who 'pretends only to learning, buys titles, and nothing else of books in him' is only an extreme case of the foppery that pressed on 'polite learning', and continued to press on it through the eighteenth century. Dr Alice Walker's detailed study of the reading of Thomas Lodge makes the point that in Lodge's work 'full value is given to anything that bore the hall-mark of Greece or Rome, while greater debts to more modern writers are passed by unacknowledged'. Many of Lodge's references turn out to have medieval sources – the same is true of Thomas Dekker – but this is revealed to the researcher not to the reader.

Shakespeare's 'classicism' cannot be wholly described in these terms. Dr Farmer, anxious to disprove Shakespeare's direct acquaintance with the classics, quoted Bishop Hurd to the effect that

they who are in such astonishment at the learning of Shakespeare forget that the Pagan imagery was familiar to all the poets of his time; and that abundance of this sort of learning was to be picked up from almost every book that he could take into his hands.

This is unsatisfactory; it does not allow for the extent to which Shakespeare's allusions are submerged in the context which they serve. Shakespeare was neither a flamboyant name-dropper nor a scholar in any modern sense; but he was not either the simple representative of 'Nature' that seventeenth and eighteenth century criticism made of him (in antithesis to Jonson). His work is erected on a consciousness of literary conventions and literary methods, derived from the study of the classics in Grammar School. Classical allusion was not simply a decoration to his style, but an integral part (however derived) of a whole mode of writing. Moreover it is reasonably certain that his 'small latin' included an ability to get sense out of works not translated, and a continuing memory of some texts that he read in Latin. This ability does not seem to have deserted him at any point in his career, for as late as *The Tempest* (v. i. 33 ff.) he can augment Golding's translation of Ovid by reference to the original (or by memory of it).

But the onset of Neo-classicism made it increasingly difficult to see Shakespeare's Renaissance skills as connected with the 'real' classics. As early as 1640 Leonard Digges – the stepson of the executor of Shakespeare's will – made it his peculiar glory that

> Nature only helped him, for look through
> This whole book thou shalt find he doth not borrow
> One phrase from Greeks, nor Latins imitate,
> Nor once from vulgar languages translate.

On the most literal level this seems not to be true. Moreover I suspect that in the period when Shakespeare started writing it would not have seemed possible as praise. Francis Meres, writing in 1598, seems closer to the actual relationship between Shakespeare and the classics:

As the soul of Euphorbus was thought to live in Pythagoras, so the sweet witty soul of Ovid lives in mellifluous and honey-tongued Shakespeare.

In this view of the matter the classical author is still an influence and an authority; but his power is derived from his capacity to release Shakespeare's own faculties. Renaissance schoolmasters insisted that the end of imitation was to learn to make something of one's own; and Shakespeare's classicism seems best regarded in these terms of creative affinity. The explicit presence of Ovid is most noticeable in Shakespeare's early work; but the Ovidian characteristics – the facility and copiousness of mellifluous rhetoric and of verbal wit – remain Shakespearian throughout his career.

A COMMUNAL CREATIVENESS

These methods of acquiring knowledge did not cease to seem appropriate when the reading moved away from classical to modern texts – or modern experiences; we remember how Hamlet calls out for his table-book when he learns from the ghost that 'one may smile, and smile, and be a villain'. The authors of the period shared a common school-experience and a common style of learning. Even more important, they shared a common world of creative methods. The acquisitiveness they had learned in relation to Cicero or Virgil, and the common stock of adages, similes, apophthegms, jests, situations they all acquired at second-hand – these led to a communal creativeness in which copying from one another or censuring the inventions of another were part of the artist's life. And nowhere does this community of creativeness seem more important than in the drama. To most of them the drama seemed (and was) of ephemeral worth. In many cases several dramatists worked together, often under great pressure of time. It was a frankly commercial area of writing, designed for quick effects and quick profits. Sequels and continuations abounded; formulae that worked well were liable to be worked to death. Moreover several of the most successful dramatists were also actors; the experience of acting in other men's plays was obviously one way of absorbing their techniques. We should not forget this mode of absorption when we think about Shakespeare's 'reading'. Undoubtedly he learned more about plays by living among players and playwrights than he did from any other source. Nor should we forget the amount that Shakespeare copied from himself. The relationship of *Twelfth Night* to *The Comedy of Errors* and to *The Two Gentlemen of Verona* is a good example, which has been skilfully explored by L. G. Salingar and by Harold Jenkins.

This community of creative interests, this absence of search either for originality of material or fidelity to individual experience – this was a European rather than an English phenomenon. And it was not only jests and adages that swelled the teeming folio collections of the period. Stories attracted the collector no less, and 'good' stories appear throughout Europe in one collection after another. Take the slander story which forms the basis of the Hero/Claudio plot in *Much Ado About Nothing*. This appears in two of the great poetic collections of stories – Ariosto's *Orlando Furioso* and Spenser's *Faerie Queene*. It also appears in prose in Bandello's *Novelle* (1554), in Belleforest's *Histoires Tragiques* (1574) – translated from Bandello – in Whetstone's *Rocke of Regard* (1576), in Peter Beverley's poem *Ariodanto and Jenevra* (1566). Presumably it appeared also in a lost play, *Ariodante and Genevra*, acted at court in 1583. Another lost play, acted in 1575, may have been based on Bandello's version. In addition there are various Italian plays on the same subject. The source-hunter is faced by an embarrassing wealth of potential sources, and only minutiae (often untrustworthy) can suggest preferences. Sometimes indeed the author seems to have been well aware of the variety of tellings to which the tale was liable and to have used the dialectic that is thus set up as part of the imaginative world of the play. Shakespeare's *Troilus and Cressida*, for example, may be seen as the product of a collision between the medieval versions of the Troy story (Chaucer, Lydgate, Caxton all seem to have contributed) and Renaissance handlings of the same material, such as Chapman's Homer, Robert Greene's *Euphues his Censure to Philautus* together with (perhaps) the thirteenth book of Ovid's *Metamorphoses*. It is worth noting that Shakespeare seems to have been more assiduous in collecting variant sources than were his fellows. Kenneth Muir remarks: 'Shakespeare, as a general rule, took more pains than his contemporaries in the collection of source material.'

SHAKESPEARE'S HISTORY

One of the recurrent problems for the modern critic dealing with Elizabethan writings is to define what 'originality' can mean inside the framework of strictly traditional ways of creating literature. Shakespeare's use of the best-known books of the period, the Bible (in both the Bishops' and the Geneva versions) and the official Homilies (appointed to be read regularly in all churches) gives a good example of the way his mind seems to have held a great reservoir of stories and phrases and ideas, always available and yet never determining his thinking. His handling of multiple sources and the freedom this gives him for a creative use of source material should also be noted. Another example of his originality, more easily understandable in modern terms, can be seen in the divergence from traditional play-material he seems to have made when he turned (very early) from the classics he read at school to the chronicles of his own country. This strongly suggests a man following his own bent rather than his schoolmaster.

So long as it was supposed that Shakespeare had begun his career with plays that were made out of other men's imaginings it could not be supposed that he was a serious and *original* reader of the chronicles. But when *The Contention betwixt the two famous houses of York and Lancaster* (1594) and *The True Tragedy of Richard Duke of York* (1595) were shown not to be the sources of Shakespeare's *Henry VI* plays but derivatives from them, the way was open for F. P. Wilson's hypothesis: 'for all we know there were no popular plays on English history before the Armada and Shakespeare may have been the first to write one'. This has important implications for a review of Shakespeare's reading; it means that Shakespeare may have been the first man to make serious use of the chronicles, as he is the only dramatist to make sustained use of them.

When Shakespeare picked up the 1587 edition of Holinshed's chronicles he made himself heir to continuous and cumulative labour of more than seventy years. It is not without significance that this was in the main citizen labour. That the knowledge of the past is a key to the present and that the observation of great events teaches immediate lessons – these were attitudes easily assimilated by a mass audience, and there is no reason to suppose that Shakespeare did not share them. His work in English history should be seen as the crown of that bourgeois effort that runs through Fabyan, Hall, Stowe and Holinshed.

What Shakespeare did not find in the chronicles but had to draw out of his creative imagination was unity of theme and structure in individual plays, a power of balancing cause against cause and individual against individual. T. W. Baldwin has argued at great length that Shakespeare's debt to his schooldays was not only a knowledge of authors but also a knowledge of rhetorical and constructive methods, based on a study of the *Ars Poetica* and Terence and of their commentators. The skill already in Shakespeare's possession at the time of writing the first four history plays seems to bear this out.

The process of writing nine history plays did not leave Shakespeare's reading of history entirely unaffected. As he moves back in time from the chaos of the Wars of the Roses into the more ordered period that set up the conflict, he seems to become more concerned with the private lives of the public figures, with personal entanglements and alternative systems of value. But an exploration of the tension between integrity and power could not be taken very far in the terms provided by Hall and Holinshed; Shakespeare's interests drive him, almost inevitably, from the history that the chroniclers purvey (what happened when) to the history that is told by 'that grave learned philosopher and historiographer, Plutarch of Chaeronea' (as Sir Thomas North calls him). Plutarch describes his own intent as:

not to write histories, but only lives. For the noblest deeds do not always show men's virtues and vices; but oftentimes a light occasion, a word or some sport, makes men's natural dispositions appear more plain than the famous battles...

(*Life of Antonius*)

Plutarch provides Shakespeare with a dramatic framework that seems to fit his purpose more completely than anything else he ever used. The plays he bases on Plutarch – *Julius Caesar, Coriolanus, Antony and Cleopatra* – are more continuously faithful to their source than any other plays in Shakespeare.

OTHER SOURCE MATERIALS

As early as 1582 Stephen Gosson, playwright turned stage-scourge, characterized the favourite source materials of the contemporary theatre:

I may boldly say it because I have seen it that the *Palace of Pleasure*, the *Golden Ass*, the *Ethiopian History*, *Amadis of France*, the *Round Table*, bawdy comedies in Latin, French, Italian and Spanish have been thoroughly ransacked to furnish the playhouses in London.

(*Plays Confuted in Five Actions*)

By the time Shakespeare was an established dramatist the list had been modified a little, but not really changed. Medieval Romance (*Amadis de Gaule*) and Greek Romance (the *Aethiopica*) had begotten hybrid forms of romantic narrative, and it is from these (Greene's *Pandosto*, Lodge's *Rosalynde*, Montemayor's *Diana*, Sidney's *Arcadia*) that Shakespeare derives his plots. Shakespeare certainly knew the *Aethiopica*; and he turns to another classical romance for the story of *Pericles*; but he shows no interest in medieval Romance though it is like enough that he knew *Guy of Warwick* and the *Amadis de Gaule* (from which he may have taken the names of Florizel and Perdita). William Painter's *Palace of Pleasure* remained a favourite source throughout the period; but the novelle reached Shakespeare in a range wider than Painter's selection; it seems probable that he drew on Italian texts of *Il Pecorone* (for *The Merchant of Venice*), of Giraldi Cinthio's *Hecatommithi* (for *Othello*), and of Boccaccio (for the wager plot in *Cymbeline*). He may, of course, have turned to French translations of the Italian; the French puns in *Love's Labour's Lost* suggest a fair facility in that language.

The third element in Gosson's list – 'bawdy comedies' – also lasted into Shakespeare's day as an important class of source material, but again in a modified form. By the last decade of the century the comic form of erotic intrigue, to which I take it Gosson is referring, had been largely naturalized, in novelle as well as in plays. Shakespeare had no need to read Ariosto's *Suppositi* when he could find the Bianca plot of *The Taming of the Shrew* already englished in Gascoigne's *Supposes*. None the less John Manningham's famous comment on *Twelfth Night* indicates that as late as 1602 there remained in educated circles in England a lively awareness of European comedy:

At our feast we had a play called *Twelfth Night or What You Will*, much like *The Comedy of Errors* or *Menechmi* in Plautus, but most like and near to that in Italian called *Inganni*.

The plot of *Gl' Ingannati* (1531), to which Manningham is probably referring, could have been known to Shakespeare through the French *Les Abuseẓ* (1543), or the Latin *Laelia* which was performed in Cambridge in 1547 and again in 1595. Alternatively it might have reached him in Bandello's novella version, or in Belleforest's translation of Bandello, or in Barnaby Rich's story in *Riche's Farewell to Military Profession* (1581), probably based on Belleforest.

The status of 'old plays' is one that has much vexed the problem of Shakespeare's sources. As noted above it was at one time supposed that Shakespeare had begun his career as a botcher of other men's plays. This not only seemed to fit the textual evidence (as interpreted at that point) but even more compellingly it tallied with the image of a Shakespeare who relied on nature rather than art. The desire to protect our national bard from too much learning, to avoid the Casaubon-like image of a studious collator of texts, a collector of evidences, a burrower among manuscripts, has often led the signs of these activities in the extant plays to be laid at the door of an 'old play'. The 'old playwright' can then take up the mask of Casaubon, and Shakespeare can revert to the ideal outlined in 'Dr Furnivall's golden words':

I see a square-built yet lithe and active fellow, with ruddy cheeks, hazel eyes and auburn hair, as full of life as an egg is full of meat, impulsive, inquiring, sympathetic; up to any fun and daring; into scrapes and out of them with a laugh; making love to all the girls; a favourite wherever he goes – even with the prigs and fools he mocks, etc.

(Introduction to the 'Leopold' Shakespeare)

Dr Dover Wilson has discovered evidence, he believes, that *Richard II* contains information derived from Hall's chronicle, Holinshed, Samuel Daniel's *Civil Wars*, Berners' translation of Froissart, the manuscript play of *Woodstock*, and two other historical manuscripts in French. He is unwilling to believe that Shakespeare read all these, and so he saddles another with the task:

Was Shakespeare a profound historical scholar or merely the reviser of such a scholar's play?...He may have dipped into the opening paragraphs of Hall or turned up Holinshed here and there...His unknown predecessor [sc. the 'old playwright'], soaked in the history of England, had read the chronicles for him and had digested what they had to say upon the downfall of Richard II into a play-book...are we not justified in supposing, from everything we know about him, that Shakespeare followed the line of least resistance, whenever he could?

'Old plays' have a further attraction for the modern critic of Shakespeare: they help to explain the 'carelessness' of much of Shakespeare's dramaturgy (when measured by Ibsenite standards) and so exempt Shakespeare from full responsibility for plays that the critic can only approve in part. *Hamlet* is the classic instance of this. It is known from Nashe's preface to Greene's *Menaphon* (1589) that a Hamlet play existed at that point; but the extant *Hamlet* cannot have been written before 1600. The ghost of the *Ur-Hamlet* haunts our sense of the

63

play; it is difficult to deal honestly with the actual body of the text when this invisible double is so available for blame.

The cases of *King Lear* and *Measure for Measure* are less dangerous to discuss, for the old plays have survived, and we can see what Shakespeare has made of them. *The True Chronicle History of King Leir and his three Daughters* was certainly known to Shakespeare; but it provided no more than a general outline of one possible route through the story. It contains no Fool, no madness, no Poor Tom (who is derived, of course, like the rest of the Gloucester plot, from Sidney's *Arcadia*), no storm, no banishment or disguise for Kent. Cordelia wins the battle at the end; the wicked dukes and the wicked daughters run away; Lear and Cordelia are restored to power and happiness. *King Lear* is nearest to the old play in the opening scene, but even here Shakespeare abandons the credible motivations of the source and gives a quite different quality to the action. It is as if Shakespeare had read or remembered the old play in the context of the other versions of the Lear story – in Holinshed, in *The Mirror for Magistrates*, in Spenser, perhaps even in the context of the recent scandal of Brian Annesley and his three daughters (the youngest called Cordell). But most of all he seems to have seen all these in terms of a vision of what they could come to mean, and so to have combined and remembered (drawing in improbable 'sources' like Samuel Harsnet's *Declaration of Egregious Popish Impostures* (1603)) and made what he willed out of what he found.

Whetstone's *Promos and Cassandra*, the 'old play' behind *Measure for Measure* is again placed by Shakespeare in the context of the many other versions of the story available to him. He changed fundamental aspects of the plot, making Isabella a novice and sparing her any defilement in the bed of Angelo. To this end he invented the figure and the stratagem of Mariana. Not only so, but by repeating the motif of the substituted victim not only for Claudio but also for Barnardine he gives it a thematic importance it does not have in any of the sources. The pretended departure of the Duke, and his return to observe the vices he suspects, is also new. Shakespeare may have got the idea from Middleton's *The Phoenix* or Marston's *The Fawn*; but he chose to apply it to this story, and he augmented the effect by making the disguise that of a friar and confessor, largely because of a leading idea which controlled the selection and connection of all the elements involved. The interrelation of mercy and justice is something which can be seen to lie latent and half-buried in the turgid rhetoric of *Promos and Cassandra*. It was no doubt this that attracted Shakespeare to the story. But in working out a structure which would release the dramatic potential of this theme, in its political, personal and theological aspects, he was obliged to recast entirely the relationship of the parts. The 'old play' is like the grain in the wood which may suggest to the carver the contours his chisel will follow, but whose 'meaning' is his invention and entirely at his discretion.

SHAKESPEARE'S CONTEMPORARY READING

It is one thing to note that Shakespeare was well read in contemporary English writing – in the works of Lyly and Marlowe and Greene, and Daniel and Chapman and Sidney; most of these were colleagues whose innovations were tied into his professional life as his innovations were tied into theirs; but the question whether or not Shakespeare 'kept up' with contemporary intellectual life in the larger sense raises quite different issues. This was, of course, a European culture, though by Shakespeare's time most of the basic books were available in English. Once again the question of actual reading is difficult to prove, and seems less important than a general acquaintance with the kind of material involved. If Shakespeare is not to be seen as a learned man, reading many books, remembering what they contain, being led from one reference to another, comparing what different authors say about similar problems, synthesizing their approaches, we must suppose he reached the same point by a different and less probable route – by living inside the intellectual problems of his own age and working out possible attitudes to them in splendid isolation (or in talk with any real intellectuals he happened to know). Certainly (and this is what matters) his dramatic conflicts reflect intellectual concerns that other men in his period focussed upon through books. The plays in the period of *Hamlet*, *Julius Caesar* and *Troilus and Cressida* show men having to make their heroism out of the accidents and insufficiencies of real experience, precisely in the manner of Montaigne:

> To whom are Caesar and Alexander beholding for that infinite greatness of their renown, but to fortune?...A man is not always upon the top of the breach, nor in the front of an army, in the sight of his general, as upon a stage. A man may be surprised between a hedge and a ditch...
>
> (II, xvi, 'Of Glory')

Does this mean that Shakespeare had read Montaigne? The germ of much of it is in Plutarch, and we know that Shakespeare had been reading Plutarch. Did Shakespeare, reading Plutarch as Montaigne read Plutarch, and responding to Plutarch's view of heroism as Montaigne responded to it, push Plutarch's view in precisely the direction that Montaigne had already followed? It is quite possible; and we cannot prove it true or untrue. The problem of the Ghost in *Hamlet*, as Dover Wilson has unravelled it, implies awareness of a Renaissance controversy about the status of ghosts. Which of the controversialists had Shakespeare read (if any)? We do not know. It is fairly clear that Edmund's soliloquy on bastardy comes from Ortensio Landi's 'paradox in the defence of bastardy'; but what understanding of libertine thought drove Shakespeare to fasten on 'besides it seemeth as a certainty that nature hath some peculiar respect of bastards' as the key to a coherent libertine philosophy? Had he been reading Montaigne or Machiavelli or Lipsius or Bodin? We do not know.

It seems inevitable, however, that the modern critic should act as if Shakespeare knew these authors, drawing on them to expand the meaning of his intellectual positions and academic conflicts. Their eloquence helps to involve the modern reader in what Shakespeare did not bother to say completely; but there is a corresponding danger that we may over-intellectualize both the plays and the author, implying that the plays were written to exemplify the intellectual positions they contain, or that Shakespeare read up this material to give himself ideas. It seems more proper to suppose that Shakespeare read Montaigne and others because they dealt with matters that already fascinated him, because he took an active part in the intellectual life of his time, seeking challenge or confirmation. Who would read through Harsnet's *Declaration of Egregious Popish Impostures* just to give a few devils names like Flibbertigibbet or Hoppididance? We must suppose, I think, that Shakespeare read widely, perhaps desultorily, but with a keen exploratory interest in the intellectual world in which he moved and to which he contributed.

5

SHAKESPEARE AND THE
ENGLISH LANGUAGE

RANDOLPH QUIRK

In this chapter we shall be concerned less with the facts of language than with attempting to establish the kind of language study that is most significant for students of Shakespeare. The title seeks to dissociate itself on the one hand from the 'language of Shakespeare's time' (which might concern contemporary archives of a remote area having no necessary connection with Shakespeare), and equally on the other hand from the 'language of Shakespeare' (which too often seems to imply that the poet is a sort of linguistic island). It should be superfluous to point out that the language of Shakespeare is an amalgam of the language that Shakespeare found around him – together with what he made of it. And these need to be painstakingly separated for the intelligent appraisal of Shakespeare to an extent that is quite unnecessary for the intelligent appraisal of Yeats or Eliot or Pinter. In other words, over and above the dense complexities that must have been difficult for the Elizabethans too, there are for us in reading Shakespeare difficulties that did not exist in Shakespeare's own time. These are paradoxically aggravated by our very familiarity with the plays: as witness our 'institutionalizing' some expressions in a usage as foreign to Shakespeare as Spenser's *derring do(e)* was to Chaucer. When Iago pretends to relieve Othello's feelings with the assurance that Cassio had spoken his passionate words to Desdemona only in his sleep, Othello says 'But this denoted a foregone conclusion' (III, iii, 432) and however carefully we have studied Elizabethan English, it is very hard for us to remember in the theatre that this does not mean what we have since taken the phrase *foregone conclusion* to mean. And Iago goes on, ' 'Tis a shrewd doubt, though it be but a dream,' using *shrewd* in the sense 'grave, serious' which is now archaic. The extent to which we love Shakespeare (as we love the Authorized Version) for the familiar but exalted language is a measure of our inability to respond to Shakespeare as his contemporaries did. We miss the chance of sharing an Elizabethan audience's savouring of old and new, slang and formal, pompous or fashionable, hackneyed or daring: the chance therefore of achieving the shock of pleasure comparable with what is possible for us in hearing, say, *Under Milk Wood*. But not only that: we are actually in danger of not grasping what is said. Let us remember, for example, that in the very frequent word-play, it is often the case that one of the meanings is dead and hence, for us, no word-play at all:Leontes' words to his little son (*The Winter's Tale* I, ii, 123), 'We must be neat – not neat, but cleanly', will illustrate this; he replaces *neat* because of its bovine sense which suggests horns and hence cuckoldry.

It is important, therefore, to study the language of Shakespeare's time and then to distinguish Shakespeare's language within it. But even this is to proceed too fast. There is an important consideration which must occupy us between these two, and that is Shakespeare's interest in and reaction to the language around him: narrowly – his interest in the linguistic fashions and controversies of his time, and more broadly – his interest in the nature of language itself. What we need is thus a study involving a three-fold distinction:

(1) English as it was about 1600;
(2) Shakespeare's interest in his language;
(3) Shakespeare's unique use of English.

In speaking of Shakespeare's 'unique' use of English it will be realized that one is speaking in linguistic terms and not in bardolatry. Every individual has a unique *parole*, a unique realization of what is possible in the language of his time and place. But at the same time this is not to deny that the *parole* of some individuals is more interesting than that of others: William Shakespeare's than Nahum Tate's, for example.

Now the language of any period can be considered as comprising three aspects: *vocabulary* – the word-stock; *grammar* – the organisation of vocabulary into sentences; and thirdly *transmission* – the means of transmitting language from one person to another, either directly by the sounds of speech or indirectly by the marks of written representation.

In many respects the English of 1600 has remained unchanged in all three aspects. Many words sound the same, and are spelt the same; many grammatical patterns have remained unchanged; many words have stayed in use and in the same use, that is, with the same meaning. Our reason for studying the language of 1600, however, is that in many respects the language has changed quite sharply, and we are confronted by two difficulties. The first is the discipline of recognizing these differences. The second is the much more acute difficulty of deciding whether these differences are purely those between our time and 1600 (features which would not seem striking to Shakespeare's audience) or whether they are differences which result from Shakespeare's creativeness (and which would therefore seem individual in his own time).

So far as transmission is concerned, the complications are both less and more troublesome. Less because – *pace* those critics who have written about individual poets' 'voices' – it is doubtful whether much can be done to distinguish an author's pronunciation – still less *voice quality* – from that of his time in general. Here is one area, in fact, where confusion has been perpetuated through such terms as 'Shakespeare's pronunciation' – even used as the title of an important book – where little attempt is made to distinguish Shakespeare from his time and where mainly the latter is meant. In addition, these problems are less troublesome, one might suggest, because it is equally doubtful whether a great deal is to be gained from a closer knowledge of transmission differences. Now that we have the technical ability to put on a play in roughly the pronunciation of 1600, the desirability of so doing has become less apparent. Since so many of the features of Elizabethan pronunciation have remained in twentieth-century use with utterly different sociological connotations, it is exceedingly difficult to avoid farcical overtones in ways that do not arise with original versions in French or German, or even in Chaucerian English.

The complications are *more* troublesome inasmuch as the two modes of transmission – sound and spelling – are necessarily confounded in dealing with an earlier time where the language is couched (as to substance) in only one of these. And while both spellings and sounds have changed, they have not changed in the same ways and we obviously cannot infer the sound changes from the spelling ones. Editing and interpretative scholarship have gained (and undoubtedly can continue to gain) from the close study of both aspects of transmission. We would rarely think of accepting an emendation today without close reference to the ways in which a given word was spelt in 1600 and the ways in which that spelling could have given rise – whether from manuscript or from print – to the corruption that we suspect. And the study of the sounds, despite the spellings, has led to a far fuller knowledge – particularly of word-play: 'I am here,' says Touchstone to the bucolic Audrey, 'I am here with thee and thy goats, as the most capricious poet, honest Ovid, was among the Goths' (*As You Like It* III, iii, 4). The connection between *goats* and *capricious* on the one hand and *Goths* on the other is obscured alike by Elizabethan spelling, our own spelling, and our modern pronunciation. It is only when we know that the pronunciation of *Goth* was different in Shakespeare's time that the full connection, the full range of the pun, can become apparent. Spelling and modern pronunciation disguise a pun similarly in Hotspur's 'That roan shall be my throne' (*1 Henry IV* II, iii, 67); cf. Kökeritz, pp. 320 f, Dobson, p. 1010.

To turn now to grammar, we find here very great and significant differences from the habits of our own time, but at least we are helped by the fact that they are for the most part obvious to us. They are not obscured by spelling as in transmission or by continuity of form as with vocabulary. Not usually, at any rate but there are snares here too, even in so seemingly innocent a form as *his*. In *Hamlet*, III, iii, the King's soliloquy presents him considering the relative ease with which justice can be evaded in 'the corrupted currents of this world'. But, he goes on (60–2),

> 'tis not so above:
> There is no shuffling; there the action lies
> In his true nature.

During the summer of 1966, at the Stratford production by Peter Hall, I heard the player heavily emphasize *his*, apparently under the impression (and certainly conveying the impression to the audience) that the reference was to God's nature, thus convicting Shakespeare at once of woolly expression and bad theology, if not of actual nonsense. Yet *his* as the genitive of *it* (here referring to *action*) was a contemporary commonplace, however much the salt has subsequently lost his savour. Abbot dismisses the point as too well-known to merit more than a single line, though he spends a page examining exceptions such as *its* and *it*.

Scarcely less firmly 'trodden under foot of men' is our former awareness of another pronominal usage, the distinction between *you* and *thou*, though many studies have been published on this point, some of them noted below (p. 266). Even when we are intellectually aware of the distinction, however, it is hard to school ourselves to the appropriate reaction when we are in the theatre, and in any case there remain misconceptions among scholars themselves. It is often said that the old singular and plural are used in Shakespeare as they are used in Chaucer: and this is quite untrue; it is often said that in 1600 *you* was polite, formal usage but *thou* was familiar or insulting. This is a gross oversimplification: cf. McIntosh, Mulholland. The modern linguistic concept of contrast operating through *marked* and *unmarked* members can give us a truer picture. *You* is usually the stylistically unmarked form: it is not so much 'polite' as 'not impolite'; it is not so much 'formal' as 'not informal'. It is for this reason that *thou* can operate in such a wide variety of contrasts with it. At one extreme we have the solemnity and formality of religious discourse as in Edmund's 'Thou, Nature, art my goddess; to thy law My services are bound' (*King Lear* I, ii, 1 f). Then again we have the very antonym of this in pure contempt: there is Sir Toby's advice to Sir Andrew Aguecheek in drafting the challenge to his rival, 'Taunt him with the license of ink; if thou thou'st him some thrice, it shall not be amiss' (*Twelfth Night* III, ii, 40 f). But we need to notice that in this instance the device draws attention to the fact that while Andrew and Fabian are using the unmarked *you* to each other and to Sir Toby, Sir Toby is using *thou* to Sir Andrew with more than a suggestion of the contempt he is advising Sir Andrew to use with the count's serving man. It is important to realize that it is not Sir Toby's use of *thou* as such which conveys his lack of respect; it is the fact that he is doing so in a social context which makes it appropriate for other speakers to use *you*. If we compare the exchanges between Falstaff and Prince Hal in *1 Henry IV*, we see sharply different values given to *thou* because the contrasts in which it operates are different. Both pass back and forth between the unmarked *you* and the marked *thou* of anger or intimacy: but there is no distancing between them in the pronoun usage and so no social opposition enters the situation. At a given moment both are using either *you* (as in Hal's 'How now, woolsack! What mutter you?' and Falstaff's 'You Prince of Wales!...Are you not a coward?' II, iv, 127 ff) or else, as a little later in the same scene, they are both using *thou* (Falstaff's 'Dost thou hear me, Hal?' and the Prince's 'Ay, and mark thee too, Jack' *ibid.* 202).

The importance of the active contrast betwen *you* and *thou* is brought out excellently in the first scene of *King Lear*. Kent, Gloucester, Edmund and Lear all use *you* in speaking to each other: as we should expect. Goneril, Regan and Cordelia address their father as *you* – again as we should expect. Lear addresses Goneril and Regan as *thou*, and again – from father to daughter – this is what we should expect. Against this background of perfect decorum and the fully expected, it should no doubt come as a surprise to us that Lear addresses Cordelia at first as *you*: 'what can you say to draw / A third more opulent than your sisters?' (I, i, 84 f). So also 93 f. It seems unlikely that these uses of *you(r)* are without significance in indicating a special feeling that Lear has for the girl he calls 'our joy', who has been, as France says, Lear's 'best object', the argument of his praise, the balm of his age, the best, the dearest (*ibid.* 214–6). When, however, he is shocked by what he takes to be her lack of love, he uses *thou* – not now the *thou* of father to daughter but the *thou* of anger: 'But goes thy heart with this?' 'Thy truth, then, be thy dower!' (104, 107). This is what is meant by saying the importance lies in *active contrast*. Although *you* is the general unmarked form beside which the use of *thou* is conspicuous, the position is that in a relationship where *thou* is expected, *you* can likewise be in contrast and conspicuous. This becomes important again and again in the scenes that follow: Lear grows cool to Goneril

and the change is reflected in the use of *you*: 'Are you our daughter?'
'Your name, fair gentlewoman?' (I, iv, 218, 235), and he turns to
Regan with his customary affectionate paternal *thou* for these two
daughters: 'Beloved Regan, Thy sister's naught' (II, iv, 131 f). The
Fool addresses the disguised Kent as *you*; Regan conspiring with
Goneril's steward expresses her ultimate acknowledgement of their
partnership by coming down the intimacy scale from *you* to *thou*:
'So fare you well...Fare thee well' (IV, v, 36, 40).

If it is only with difficulty that we today can respond to this contrast
of *you* and *thou*, our sensitivity is still less in relation to the use of the
second person pronoun with imperatives. The pronoun may have
subject form or object form or it may be absent, and in some cases – 17,
according to Millward – all three possibilities can occur with the same
verb:

> Come thou on my side. (*Richard III* I, iv, 263)
> Come thee on. (*Antony and Cleopatra* IV, vii, 16)
> Come on my right hand. (*Julius Caesar* I, ii, 213).

While it would be idle to pretend that these three forms of imperative
were always carefully distinguished in meaning at this time, we must
not assume that they were usually synonymous. Leaving out of account
reflexive use like *calm thee*, it would seem that, beside an 'unmarked'
imperative without any pronoun, the form with *thou* was emphatic;
this is frequently clear from the metre or the context, as when the
Second Murderer refuses to profit from the death of Clarence:

> Take thou the fee, and tell him what I say. (*Richard III* I, iv, 275)

The pronoun subject becomes especially contrastive when the *do*
auxiliary is also used, as when Queen Margaret begs for death:

> What, wilt thou not? Then, Clarence, do it thou.
> ...sweet Clarence, do thou do it. (*3 Henry VI* V, v, 71, 73)

Or, in a different vein, Falstaff's plea:

> Do not thou, when thou art king, hang a thief. (*1 Henry IV* I, ii, 60)

On the other hand, the imperative with the objective form of the
pronoun (which may be better explained as an unstressed form of the
subject pronoun) seems rather to seek the personal involvement of
the addressee. We may compare Polonius' farewell to his son:

> Farewell; my blessing season this in thee (*Hamlet* I, iii, 81)

with the Ghost's to his son:

> Fare thee well at once...
> Adieu, adieu, adieu! Remember me. (*ibid.* v, 88, 91)

It is naturally especially common with verbs used to summon attention, such as *look* and *hark*: for example,

> But hear thee, Gratiano:
> Thou art too wild.... (*The Merchant of Venice* II, ii, 165 f)

Mention has been made of the *do* auxiliary (p. 72). Shakespeare witnessed the increasing association of this auxiliary with questions, negation and emphasis (*Do you go? I don't go, I DO go*), but for the most part a choice remained which could be used for stylistic contrast. As Mrs Salmon (1965) has pointed out, Jacques Bellot was among Shakespeare's contemporaries one of those most plainly aware of the use of *do* to confer a weighty and sonorous rotundity, observing that people 'doe adde commonly the verb Faire, before the other verbes, for the replenishing and sounding of their tongue with more grace' (*Le Maistre d'Escole Anglais*). It is in this knowledge that we must savour Falstaff's coloured rhetoric when he plays the King:

> This pitch, as ancient writers do report, doth defile.
> (*1 Henry IV* II, iv, 400)

or when he exults in Mistress Page's passion for him:

> O, she did so course o'er my exteriors with such a greedy intention that the
> appetite of her eye did seem to scorch me up like a burning-glass.
> (*The Merry Wives of Windsor* I, iii, 62 ff)

The purpose has been to show that even the minutiae of grammar present important differences in Elizabethan English; it goes without saying that such differences are no less important in larger matters such as clause and sentence structure. But it is time we glanced at the remaining aspect of language, vocabulary. The difficulties here – as in transmission – are often disguised. That is to say, we really do not come upon many entirely strange words in Shakespeare that hoist a danger signal warning us to consult Onions or the *N.E.D.* When Salerio in *The Merchant of Venice* says 'Slubber not business for my sake' (II, viii, 39), we are compelled to look up *slubber* ('treat carelessly'). Later in the play, Portia says that she speaks too long, 'to peize the time' (III, ii, 22), meaning to weigh it down and make it slow. The problem of entirely strange words is not, of course, to be underrated, and there are plenty in Shakespeare 'stranger' than *slubber* and *peize*: *chopine* (a kind of shoe) and *eisel* (vinegar) occur in *Hamlet*, *kecksy* (a wild plant) and *sutler* (camp-follower) in *Henry V*. And generations of editors, let alone readers, have been puzzled by Petruchio's

> Sit down, Kate, and welcome. Soud, soud, soud, soud.
> (*The Taming of the Shrew* IV, i, 125)

Many have taken it to be a nonsense-word, part of the snatch of song that has just preceded, or an exclamation; some have preferred to emend *s* to *f*. This is a good illustration of the great scope still remaining for work on Shakespeare's problem words and Dr Hulme has argued in favour of reading *u* as *n*, the word *sonde* in the sense of 'food' having been certainly still current in the mid-fifteenth century.

But the problem of overtly strange words is less than the problem of words which disguise their strangeness. We meet a large number of words more or less familiar in their graphic substance, but with different meanings which we can easily ignore, to our loss, since very frequently the modern meaning will make some kind of sense in the Shakespearian context. For example, Polonius tells Reynaldo to 'breathe' his son's faults 'quaintly' (*Hamlet* II, i, 31) and we may link Polonius with quaintness in the modern sense without surprise; but Polonius means the insinuation to be done *artfully*. Iago's *shrewd doubt* quoted earlier would also make sense in terms of the present-day meanings, but we are the losers if we do not realize that *shrewd* means 'serious'. We are still further misled if we do not understand Edmund's 'pretence of danger' in its Elizabethan sense, 'dangerous or malicious purpose' (*King Lear* I, ii, 84). Similar examples will spring to mind: *important* often meant 'importunate', *perfection* 'performance'; *humour, frank, kind, husband, sad, safe, quick, respect* – one could make a very long list of words which are among the commonest today but whose modern meaning is, as C. S. Lewis categorized it, the 'dangerous' one when we meet them as common words also in Shakespeare.

All these differences – in transmission, grammar, and vocabulary – are part of the normal linguistic process. Similar differences can be found in comparing the language of Chaucer or of Dr Johnson with our own: change is unchanging, so to say; only the examples of linguistic change differ from comparison to comparison. But each age has its special linguistic preoccupations too: in Chaucer's time, for instance, the co-existence with a largely popular English of a largely courtly French; in Dr Johnson's the problem of reducing the language to teachable rule in the light of enlightenment and rationalism, and in the face of a growing middle class that was literate. In Shakespeare's time, too, there were special preoccupations – the post-Renaissance experimentation with language, a fluidity of linguistic fashion and a new literary self-consciousness on the part of writers in the vernacular; an ambition to achieve a literature in English to match that of the classical languages or at any rate that of French or Italian.

I have just used the word *fluidity*, but we must be cautious here. I applied it to linguistic fashion, not to the language itself. Again and again, one finds writers on Shakespeare's language describing a rule-less norm-less flux – a bright chaotic galaxy only constellated by the bard's genius, who created patterns that were entirely original and *sui generis*. We all know this to be wholly distorted, but despite our intellectual awareness of this, its effect as a piece of critical rhetoric (not to say folklore) on our imagination seems unavoidable from time to time. All languages (we must continually remind ourselves) are always in a state of flux. And when we consider the linguistic originality with which English has been used in the past eighty years by men like Hopkins, Joyce or even Dylan Thomas, we must see that the artist of our own time is no more restricted by a rule-ful, norm-ful language than Shakespeare was. The ways in which Shakespeare is seen as being defiantly independent often (if not usually) concern word-formation and in particular 'conversion' from one part of speech to another: but of course this is a property of English in all periods not merely of Shakespeare's period, still less of Shakespeare alone. Again, only specific examples of the process are Shakespeare's.

'Chaos and fire-new, unharnessed energy.' 'A buccaneering spirit in language as well as on the high seas.' Gross, romantic distortions? Not entirely, we must admit. There was less *sense of fixity* about the language in 1600 than in some other periods, and also more outspoken controversy and overt interest in the medium. The cult of the hard word as a necessity and indeed a virtue is something which runs through the whole period. *Ovids Banquet of Sence* (1595) shows Chapman delighting in obscure new words and elegant conceits; *disparent* seemingly used by no one else, appears on the second page. He says in his preface: 'that Poesie should be as perviall as Oratorie, and plainnes her speciall ornament, were the plaine way to barbarisme... it serves not a skilfull Painters turne, to draw the figure of a face onely to make knowne who it represents; but hee must lymn, give luster, shaddow, and heightning; which though ignorants will esteeme spic'd, and too curious, yet such as have the judiciall perspective, will see it hath motion, spirit, and life...Obscuritie in affection of words, and indigested concets, is pedanticall and childish; but where it shroudeth it selfe in the hart of his subiect, uttered with fitnes of figure, and expressive Epethites; with that darknes wil I still labour to be shad-dowed; rich Minerals are digd out of the bowels of the earth, not found in the superficies and dust of it.'

In 1595 we have had the fashion for augmenting the language as it flourished with Thomas Elyot, the countermovement against excess augmentation from the inkhorn as fought by Thomas Wilson and Puttenham, and now with Chapman and others the rejoinder that, yes, *affected* and *pedantic* obscurities for their own sake are to be repudiated, but a high degree of ornamentation and precision is required and to this end 'rich Minerals' must continue to be 'digd out of the bowels of the earth'.

One needs to stress this tug of war because it is commonly said that Shakespeare scorned the inkhorn, and one can cite many passages which seem to support this. 'I have receiv'd my proportion, like the Prodigious Son,' says Launce in *The Two Gentlemen of Verona* (II, iii, 3), and as Silvia says in the following scene (line 30), 'A fine volley of words' can be 'quickly shot off'. Shakespeare is aware that the unlearned can be injudiciously attracted by high-sounding language with his Hostess Quickly's *honeysuckle* for 'homicidal', *honey-seed* for 'homicide' (*2 Henry IV*, II, i, 47 f), his Dogberry and Verges, and his Costard ('welcome the sour cup of prosperity! Affliction may one day smile again': *Love's Labour's Lost* I, i, 291). Launcelot's *impertinent* (*The Merchant of Venice* II, ii, 124) confuses 'pertinent' and 'important' in its contemporary sense of 'urgent'. Benvolio mocks the Nurse by using *indite* for *invite* (*Romeo and Juliet* II, iv, 125), a malapropism elsewhere used by Hostess Quickly (*2 Henry IV* II, i, 25). But this is not to scorn augmentation and the inkhorn: there was no disagreement on this point – that the uneducated would make ridiculous errors. John Hart, the Chester Herald, had pointed this out in his *Methode* of 1570, when he gave examples such as *temporal* for 'temperate', *certisfied* for both 'certified' and 'satisfied', *dispense* for 'suspense'. It was an undoubted fact, to which George Baker had testified in 1576 (*The New Jewel of Health*), that some people, 'more curious than wyse, esteeme of nothing but that which is most rare, or in harde and unknowne languages', and we recall Don Adriano de Armado and his 'posteriors of this day', which 'the rude multitude call the afternoon' and which is an expression that seems to Holofernes 'liable, congruent, and measurable' (*Love's Labour's Lost* v, i, 76–8). Again, there was no disagreement on this: as in the passage quoted from Chapman above, the use of learned language for obscurity's sake was ridiculous and Shakespeare shows it to be so, just as he shows the ignorant *attempt* at learned language to be so. From Armado to Polonius and beyond, we have characters who draw out the thread of their verbosity finer than the staple of their argument, as Holofernes puts it (*Love's Labour's Lost* v, i, 14), and it is not only he and Nathaniel who are laughed at for having 'been at a great feast of languages and stol'n the scraps' (*ibid.* 34). Nathaniel may speak of abrogating scurrility (*Love's Labour's Lost* IV, ii, 51), Touchstone of abandoning the society of this female, 'which in the boorish' is leave the company of this woman (*As You Like It* v, i, 42 ff), and this is ridiculous. But when Macbeth likewise pairs a learned expression with its 'boorish' equivalent, as in:

> this my hand will rather
> The multitudinous seas incarnadine,
> Making the green one red,　　(II, ii, 61–3)

or earlier:

> If th' assassination
> Could trammel up the consequence, and catch,
> With his surcease, success; that but this blow
> Might be the be-all and the end-all here,　　(I, vii, 2–5)

he is not being ridiculous. Here is the inkhorn used in deadly earnest, deliberately, as an expressive virtue. And this is the position taken up, as we saw, by Chapman and this was even the ultimate position of Cheke and Wilson: augmentation was necessary, the language was deficient in aureate expression. A generation before Shakespeare was born, Skelton was pointing out that the language was so 'rude' and lacking in 'pollysshed tearmes'

> That if I wold apply
> To write ornatly
> I wot not where to finde
> Tearmes to serve my mynde.

As poets felt particularly acutely the language's need, so it was they who supplied the need most discriminatingly. Puttenham (*The Arte of English Poesie*, 1589) acknowledges the services that poets have rendered in 'their studious endevours, commendably employed in enriching and polishing their native Tongue'. Nash (*Pierce Penilesse*, 1592) praises 'the Poets of our time' for having 'cleansed our language from barbarisme' and Gervase Markham (*The Gentlemans Academie*, 1595) praises them for having given English its new 'glory and exact compendiousness'. Francis Meres lists Shakespeare and Chapman among the poets by whom 'the English tongue is mightily enriched, and gorgeouslie invested in rare ornaments and resplendent abiliments', and speaks specifically of 'Shakespeares fine filed phrase' (*Palladis Tamia*, 1598).

While Shakespeare laughed at the excesses of augmentation, therefore, he was himself deeply engaged in the process and was acknowledged to be so. He was similarly ambivalent about euphuism. There is the burlesque of Launce and Speed in *The Two Gentlemen of Verona* (for example, III, i) or of Osric (*Hamlet* v, ii). There is Falstaff: 'for though the camomile, the more it is trodden on the faster it grows, yet youth, the more it is wasted the sooner it wears' (*1 Henry IV*, II, iv, 388). Yet the forced ingenuity of symmetry and image characteristic of euphuist prose can be detected in serious verse too: in *Richard III*,

77

in *Othello*, not least in *1 Henry IV*. Two scenes after Falstaff's burlesque, we have the King speaking somewhat in the ridiculed vein:

> whereof a little
> More than a little is by much too much.
> So, when he had occasion to be seen,
> He was but as the cuckoo is in June,
> Heard, not regarded, seen, but with such eyes
> As, sick and blunted with community,
> Afford no extraordinary gaze,
> Such as is bent on sun-like majesty.　　(III, ii, 72–9)

One final facet of linguistic fashion deserves a mention. Robert Cawdrey's *Table Alphabeticall* of 1604 echoes the well-known condemnation by Thomas Wilson fifty years earlier of those who 'pouder their talke with oversea language'. The fashion has been sustained over half a century whereby 'He that commeth lately out of Fraunce, will talke French English...An other chops in with English Italienated.' Indeed, said Wilson, 'I dare sweare this, if some of their mothers were alive, thei were not able to tell what they say' (*Arte of Rhetorique*, 1553). 'The pox of such antic, lisping, affecting fantasticoes; these new tuners of accent,' says Mercutio; 'these fashion-mongers, these pardon me's' (*Romeo and Juliet* II, iv, 27, 32).

Small wonder, then, if engaged so deeply in the linguistic foibles, fashions, controversies and creativeness of his time, that Shakespeare's interest should extend also to the scepticism about the linguistic sign itself which was current if far from dominant in Elizabethan and Jacobean thought. Every man's language 'is eloquent ynough for hym self', writes a translator of Peter Ramus in 1574, countering the argument of the superiority of Latin, 'and that of others in respect of it is had as barbarous'. 'That which we call a rose By any other name would smell as sweet', and if Juliet (*Romeo and Juliet* II, ii, 43 f) cannot claim the poet's sanction any more than Falstaff with his 'What is honour? A word' (*1 Henry IV*, v, i, 132), it can be fairly claimed that they both have greater sanction than Juliet's nurse to whom primitive word-magic is attributed in 'Doth not rosemary and Romeo begin both with the same letter?' (*Romeo and Juliet* II, iv, 201).

The word-magic game is one that Cordelia refuses to play in reply to Lear's 'what can you say to draw / A third more opulent than your sisters?...mend your speech a little' (*King Lear* I, i, 85, 93); cf Mahood. It may seem ironical but it is no contradiction that the man who could use words to greatest effect was one who saw most clearly and sophisticatedly the distinction between 'words, words, mere words' and 'matter from the heart' (*Troilus and Cressida* v, iii, 108), and was able to frame so sardonic a speculation for Bolingbroke on the power of words:

> How long a time lies in one little word!
> Four lagging winters and four wanton springs
> End in a word: such is the breath of Kings.
> (*Richard II* I, iii, 213 ff)

But it is time to say a few words – and space alone forbids more – on the last leg of my proposed tripos. First, the language of Shakespeare's time; second, Shakespeare's interest in the language of his time; and only then shall we, thirdly, be in a position to attempt useful observations about his own use of the language of his time.

And how many there are to make! When all is done to get things into perspective, to see the rich texture of the language in Shakespeare's time, there is still a great deal of individuality in Shakespeare's usage. In word-formation, for instance, and particularly in verb-formation. The dynamic element in Shakespeare's clauses is characteristically the most sharply pointed, and he is particularly fond of verbs with the prefixes *be-* and *en-*. Albany tells his wife 'Bemonster not thy feature' (*King Lear* IV, ii, 63), Kent speaks of Lear's 'unnatural and be-madding sorrow' (III, i, 38), and it is worth considering the verbal force that *bemadding* has retained here beside the comparatively static, attributive value acquired by *maddening*, which was coined later. As for verbs with *en-*, one need only cite Cassio's lines in *Othello*:

> The gutter'd rocks, and congregated sands,
> Traitors ensteep'd to enclog the guiltless keel.
> (II, i, 69 f)

(or, with Kenneth Muir in the Penguin edition of 1968, *enscarped* 'abruptly shelved', in place of *ensteep'd*). And highly charged verbs emerge also from the direct-conversion process: 'The hearts That spaniel'd me at heels' (still more if with Hulme we prefer *pannelled* to Hanmer's emendation) in *Antony and Cleopatra* IV, xii, 20 f, or Edgar's tightly compressed 'He childed as I father'd' (*King Lear* III, vi, 110).

Even his noun units often have a dynamic, verbal character as we see from 'gutter'd rocks, and congregated sands' just quoted from *Othello*. This is no less noticeable in many of the image-decked nominal groups in the Sonnets: 'your own dear-purchas'd right' (Sonnet 117), 'your ne'er-cloying sweetness' (118), 'fore-bemoaned moan' (30), 'his sweet up-locked treasure' (52), 'the time-bettering days' (82), 'proud-pied April' (98), (Time's) 'bending sickle's compass' (116). And as these complex, clause-embedding modifiers may turn our minds to Hopkins, one may also cite 'the world-without-end hour' in Sonnet 57.

Perhaps because grammatical patterning had so recently been exploited *ad nauseam* in the euphuistic style, lexical patterning may be presumed to be nearer the centre of Shakespeare's interest. We may quote from Mortimer's speech to his keepers in *1 Henry VI* to illustrate what is meant:

> Weak shoulders, overborne with burdening grief,
> And pithless arms, like to a withered vine
> That droops his sapless branches to the ground.
> Yet are these feet, whose strengthless stay is numb,
> Unable to support this lump of clay,
> Swift-winged with desire to get a grave. (II, v, 10 ff)

Hardly the bard at his best, yet there is very considerable complexity in what he is attempting, a complexity in lexicology not syntax; or, rather, in that kind of 'lexical syntax' in which some modern linguists are becoming increasingly interested. *Weak* has a grammatical link (as modifier) with *shoulders*; *shoulders* is linked lexically to *burdening*, since there is a traditional collocation *burden – shoulder*; 'weak with grief' is thus achieved through the network of lexical and grammatical links. From *shoulders* to the lexically connected *arms*; but *arms* is grammatically linked to *pithless* which then lexically connects with *vine*, while conversely the grammatical modifier of *vine* (*withered*) works back to *arms* which become the *sapless branches* of the following line, though the direct lexical congruence is with *vine*. The *feet*, as part of a lexical series with *shoulders* and *arms*, have a grammatically specified *stay* which is *strengthless* and *numb*; at this point we may notice the morphological as well as semantic links between *pithless*, *sapless* and *strengthless*, the first two collocating most naturally with *vine* but (especially with the help of the third) working well with the human limbs. The *stay* has both a grammatical and a lexical link with *support*, and the latter looks back to *shoulder* and *burden* lexically as well as forward to *lump of clay*, the lexical link in addition to the grammatical one working to counteract any feeling of 'mixed' metaphor. The last line, apart from a lexical connection between *clay* and *grave*, sees a lightning antithesis to the heavily endorsed overburdened weakness of the preceding lines, an antithesis that is Mercurial in two senses as the feet become swift-winged with desire to get a grave.

Lexical congruence working through, without, or in defiance of syntactic structure is, of course, the stock machinery of imagery, and characteristically the Shakespearian image is developed in a pairing of lexical items through syntax or collocation or both. The latter – the most straightforward – is seen, for example, in the adequacy with which Ulysses' musical image is established in the words, 'untune that string' (*Troilus and Cressida* I, iii, 109). Syntax and collocation working independently produce more complex images; we may compare with the Ulysses example the following:

> Unthread the rude eye of rebellion.
> (*King John* V, iv, 11)

In addition to the grammatical (verb – object) connection between *unthread* and *eye*, there is a discontinuous lexical connection between *eye*'s premodifier *rude* and postmodifier *rebellion*, the transverse arrangement helping to remove the danger of destroying the image by an unwelcome mixture. A somewhat similar effect can be observed in

> Heaven stops the nose at it, and the moon winks
> (*Othello* IV, ii, 78)

where the two clauses are grammatically related by co-ordination, by subjects that collocate (*heaven* and *moon*) and by predicates that are lexically congruent also: closing nose and eye. But it is the transverseness of these lexical links that minimizes the incongruence in the image of heaven stopping its nose. In the following example from *As You Like It* there is a discontinuous linkage with a different arrangement:

> ...weed your better judgments
> Of all opinion that grows rank in them.　(II, vii, 45 f)

The two verbs *weed* and *grows* are lexically congruent, and to this set belongs also the complement *rank* (for *weed* and *rank*, compare *Hamlet* I, ii, 135 f; III, iv, 151 f). Nested between *weed* and *grows* are two nouns which likewise collocate; the fact that both are equally and analogously incongruent with the verbs to which they are grammatically linked (as object and subject respectively) helps to establish and empower an image that depends upon an 'unlexical' sequence.

But given the phenomenon of multiple meaning, a single lexical sign can self-collocate and produce the congruent collocation in more than one direction from itself. There is an example of this in Portia's well-known 'mercy' speech, the pivotal word being *strain'd* (*The Merchant of Venice* IV, i, 179). Shylock has just asked 'On what compulsion must I?' and so *strain'd* in Portia's reply has an obvious backward link to this: there is no compulsiveness in mercy. But then it works forward also to the dropping of the gentle rain: mercy is not filtered, drop by drop, from heaven; cf. Mahood (1957), p. 22. It is worth considering the *sullied – solid* crux in this light too (*Hamlet* I, ii,

129). Thus it would seem that the phonological experts can allow us a neutralized phonetic contrast; cf. Dobson (1968), pp. 581 ff, 592 f and notes. At the same time, the semantic span is well motivated, so that while at the point of utterance the word's relations are backwards to the pollution by the Queen's incest (cf. Clemen (1951), p. 114), thereafter it seems perverse to ignore the lexical congruity of *solid* with the *melt* that leads to *thaw, resolve,* and *dew* in the next line (cf. Mahood (1957), p. 16).

There is a more obvious 'syntactic' movement through lexical interaction when multiple meaning is allowed to emerge in the course of repetition. Leontes' reaction to *neat* may be adduced again, 'We must be neat – not neat, but cleanly' (*The Winter's Tale* I, ii, 123), in which only the first occurrence may be said to collocate with *cleanly*. But his use of *play* is a better illustration:

> Go, play, boy, play; thy mother plays, and I
> Play too; but so disgrac'd a part. . .   (*ibid.* 187 f)

The second instance of *play* is in part colloquial repetition but it is partly also the sinister turning point, a lingering over the word which releases the sexual sense (*N.E.D.* 10c) in which the third instance occurs, indicated collocationally by the female subject; the fourth instance again shows by collocation (*part*) its ironically different use.

There are of course many aspects of Shakespeare's use of English and many approaches to his language that can sharpen and enrich our reaction to the plays and poems. It would not have been practicable here to explore more than a meagre selection of the possibilities, and equally it has not seemed appropriate to attempt a wider coverage at the expense of depth. The concentration on certain facets reflects my belief that it is especially through further study of the interrelations of grammatical and lexical patterns that linguists can in the immediate future offer contributions most readily compatible with and contributory to the insights of literary scholarship.

6

SHAKESPEARE'S USE OF RHETORIC

BRIAN VICKERS

I

Rhetoric was for over two thousand years the most important discipline to anyone interested in literature. It was in existence as an art several centuries before Aristotle and it extended its influence on Western literature right up to the time of Wordsworth (see, in the Reading List, books by Abrams, Stone). It began life as a practical tool, in the law-courts, for our earliest knowledge of rhetoric is as an aid to litigation (Kennedy) and it was developed and applied to politics in Greece and still more so in Rome. The Romans took especially seriously the importance of rhetoric in education, and although they derived the principle and much of their system from Hellenistic schools (Marrou) it was thanks to their thorough establishment of the rhetorical education throughout the Roman Empire that rhetoric established itself in both secular and Christian contexts strongly enough to survive the fall of that Empire and continue in vigour through the Middle Ages (Curtius, C. S. Baldwin, Faral), indeed gathering momentum in the Renaissance partly through the separate developments in Byzantium and their influx into Florence (Bolgar). In England rhetoric was pursued with the same fervour as in other Humanist cultures (Howell) perhaps more so, because of the increasing role it played in education (Curtius, T. W. Baldwin). Indeed the English rhetoric-books of the late sixteenth century seem more inventive, more imaginative in their realization of the literary applications of rhetoric than their continental counterparts. (A concise history of rhetoric, with further references, can be found in Vickers, 1970.)

Rhetoric was rejected by the Romantic movement as an 'artificial system' which hampered the expression of individuality, and much abuse was attached to its supposedly 'rigid', 'sterile' nature. Today we still live with the post-Romantic animus to rhetoric, an animus which has passed into the language: 'rhetorical', 'oratorical', 'rhetorician', are words with ineradicable connotations of falseness and specious display. But curiously enough the same prejudice is attached to many words deriving from the drama: 'theatrical', 'stagey', 'acting'

(Barish), and I would like to suggest that while in both cases the words we use betray a certain suspicion of display we should be able to detach rhetoric from these connotations as easily as we detach the drama from them.

But the issue of 'system' needs more discussion, for unless we settle it satisfactorily there is always the danger that readers unconvinced of the literary importance of rhetoric will regard Shakespeare's indisputable mastery of that art with suspicion, and may transfer to him the unenlightened animus which they attach to rhetoric. The 'art of speech', the 'art of speaking well' was indeed developed into a system with its own conventions, but it was no more harmful to expressiveness in literature than those conventions which we all accept in the other arts, the laws of perspective in painting, the laws of harmony in music: rhetorical figures are to be regarded as artistic conventions of the same order as rhyme or metrical patterns in poetry, sonata-form or fugue in music. The paradox is that by subordinating himself to artistic conventions, to agreed limitations and shorthand modes of expression, the artist working within a traditional system was then able to achieve a freedom and spontaneity which had a universal relevance, for the language of art was understood by all. One of the fascinations of studying the development of writers using the rhetorical tradition is to trace just this process of assimilation, from an external form to something lived through, imbued with life. Some of the most knowledgeable rhetoricians have been the greatest poets: Virgil, Dante, Chaucer, Shakespeare, Racine, Herbert, Milton, Pope. Considering this fact few would want to accuse them of rigidity or sterility, and many might consider the possibility that rhetoric, instead of being a hindrance, was a creative help.

II

Although rhetoric began as a tool for public life, its relevance to literature was soon realized. The eloquence of the lawyer or orator was a quality which the poet also needed, and at a very early date (aided of course by the dominance of rhetoric in education) rhetoric was regarded as the repository of all eloquence, and both poetry and prose were equated with rhetoric and with each other. Poetry merely had the extra complication of metrics, and indeed throughout the life-span of rhetoric poetry was seldom granted an autonomous existence (fleetingly in Tasso). Hence the methods of rhetoric, originally developed for the needs of the orator in a law-court or political assembly, were adapted to literature, not always with relevance. For instance the five stages of composition were *inventio, dispositio, elocutio, pronuntiatio, memoria*: invention (that is, 'finding' one's material, usually with the corollary that one 'found' it in the various places where one had stored it, the *loci* or 'places, seats' in one's notebooks), disposition or arrangement, elocution or style, delivery and memory. Evidently the last two stages were relevant to the orator memorizing his speech and delivering it with appropriate gestures, but they were not much use to the dramatist, nor indeed were invention and disposition except in the generalized sense of the selection and ordering of plot-material. But since this 'material' was the stuff of human life, the interaction between human beings, then the various rhetorical techniques for 'invention' and structure were of little relevance.

Thus it would seem, in theory as in practice, that the relevant teaching for the poet or dramatist was that contained within *elocutio*, style. Several historians of rhetoric lament the prominence given to style in rhetorical handbooks, preferring some more 'philosophical' attitude to communication. But if one surveys the history of rhetoric it becomes evident that despite the occasional exhortations of an Aristotle, a Cicero or a Quintilian that rhetoric should become more a way of life, a culture, a public and private ethic even, rhetoric had a kind of centre of gravity which kept pulling it back towards style (Vickers, 1970). The most influential classical rhetoric-books were not Aristotle's *Rhetoric*, Cicero's *Orator*, Quintilian's *Institutes of Oratory*, but Cicero's early and schematic *de Inventione* and the pseudo-Ciceronian *Ad Herennium*, Book Four of which consists simply of a list of figures. The medieval rhetoric-books are most often organized around a list of the figures, usually taken straight from the *Ad Herennium* (Faral, C. S. Baldwin), and the most popular compilations in the Renaissance, whether continental Latin ones by Susenbrotus and Trapezuntius or English ones by Wilson, Peacham and Puttenham, gravitate towards a list of the figures which was often the most thumbed part, as surviving copies show. For nearly two thousand years what the student and budding writer most wanted from rhetoric-books was a list of the tropes and figures, set out as clearly as possible, and this fact seems to me good evidence for man's intuitive recognition that rhetoric was fundamentally different from logic or philosophy: it was a literary discipline, and it was properly concerned with the details of language and expressiveness.

Shakespeare's main interest in rhetoric lay in the tropes and schemes, and we must re-create, re-experience that interest if we are properly to understand his poetic development. This is easier said than done, for several reasons. The terminology of the figures is not their most attractive aspect, and even the rhetoricians were sometimes confused by variations of terms (Sonnino is a useful guide here). Then there are so many figures (any moderately complete list looks frightening), for since rhetoric presented a formalizing of all possible linguistic effects then a large proportion of the figures refer to rare or unusual structures. In her pioneering study, *Shakespeare's Use of the Arts of Language*, Sister Miriam Joseph assembled from various sources a list of two hundred odd figures and showed that Shakespeare indeed used them all at one time or another: but we must discriminate here, and even some one as committed to rediscovering rhetoric as I am must feel doubts concerning such peculiarities as *bdelygmia* or *onedismus*. The hundred or so figures in the *Ad Herennium* are already sufficient, and for most critical purposes a central corpus of about the forty most frequently used figures is adequate. But even these names look forbidding – *polyptoton, epanorthosis, epistrophe*. One can only plead that the Greek or Latin names are etymologically descriptive of the specific effect created by each figure and that it seems better to master the most important names rather than invent new ones or try to anglicize them (as in Puttenham's ill-fated attempt: '*Syllepsis* or the double supply', '*Parison*, or the figure of even', '*Ploce*, or the doubler'). One thing is certain, that every person who had a grammar-school education in Europe between Ovid and Pope knew by heart, familiarly, up to a hundred figures, by their right names. As Puttenham's best editors have said

A well-educated modern reader may confess without shame to momentary confusion between *Hypoʒeuxis* and *Hypoʒeugma*, but to his Elizabethan prototype the categories of the figures were, like the multiplication-tables, a part of his foundations...We are all aware of the patterning in Elizabethan verse of this period, but we are generally content to name the *genus* – balance, antithesis, repetition, and so on. The educated Elizabethan could give a name to every *species*.

(pp. lxxvff)

And although we may continue to have difficulty distinguishing the figures, even an hour's practice will make it surprisingly easy.

All rhetorical devices were thought of as deviations made from the norm of 'plain' communication (strictly conceived) for some emotional or structural purpose. These devices were divided into *tropes* and *figures* (figures were sometimes called *schemes*). A trope (or 'turn') involves a change or transference of a word's meaning: from the literal to the imaginative plane, in such devices as metaphor, allegory, irony, *litotes* (understatement), *hyperbole* (overstatement), *synecdoche* (substituting the part for the whole), *metonymy* (substituting greater for lesser). Modern criticism has rediscovered the tropes extremely well, and there are many valuable studies of Shakespeare's imagery, but the figures have yet to be generally accepted, and it is on these that I shall concentrate. The figures sometimes involve changes of meaning, but they are primarily concerned with the shape or physical structure of language, the placing of words in certain syntactical positions, their repetition in varying patterns (to make an analogy with music, tropes exist in a vertical plane, like pitch or harmony; the figures exist in a horizontal plane, like rhythm or other stress-devices). It will be convenient, perhaps, to define the most popular figures, and for convenience I take all my illustrations from *Richard III*.

First, the very familiar group of figures which create symmetrical structure, often found together. *Anaphora*, the most common of all rhetorical figures, repeats a word at the beginning of a sequence of clauses or sentences:

> Then curs'd she Richard, then curs'd she Buckingham,
> Then curs'd she Hastings.   (III, iii, 18–9)

That example also used *parison*, in which within adjacent clauses or sentences word corresponds to word (either repeating the same word – 'curs'd' – or else grouping noun with noun, adjective with adjective, etc.). A more exact use of *parison*, putting great ironic stress on the final word, is this:

> Was ever woman in this humour woo'd?
> Was ever woman in this humour won?   (I, ii, 227–8)

Both these examples increase the effect of symmetry by using *isocolon*, which gives exactly the same length to corresponding clauses, as again in the Duchess of York's catalogue of a family's distress:

> She for an Edward weeps, and so do I:
> I for a Clarence weep, so doth not she.
> These babes for Clarence weep, and so do I:
> I for an Edward weep, so do not they.   (II, ii, 82–5)

The obverse of *anaphora* is *epistrophe*, the same word ending a sequence of clauses. Shakespeare rightly chooses this figure to spotlight the sinister effect of Richard's 'planted' prophecy

> which says that G
> Of Edward's heirs the murderer shall be.   (I, i, 39–40)

As intended, suspicion falls on Clarence, who protests that the King

> hearkens after prophecies and dreams,
> And from the cross-row plucks the letter G,
> And says a wizard told him that by G

87

His issue disinherited should be;
And, for my name of George begins with G,
It follows in his thought that I am he.   (I, i, 54–9)

That is a rather special use of *epistrophe* but it conforms to the theoretical justification of the figure as stressing a word of importance. Symmetry is also invoked for *antimetabole*, which repeats words but in an inverted order:

Since every Jack became a gentleman,
There's many a gentle person made a Jack.   (I, iii, 71–2)

Next a group of figures which repeat individual words in various ways. *Ploce* is one of the most used figures of stress (especially in this play), repeating a word within the same clause or line:

...themselves the conquerors
Make war upon themselves – brother to brother,
Blood to blood, self against self.   (II, iv, 61–3)

Epizeuxis is a more acute form of *ploce*, where the word is repeated without any other word intervening:

O Pomfret, Pomfret! O thou bloody prison.   (III, iii, 8)

Epanalepsis repeats the same word at the beginning and end of the same line, as with 'themselves' in the example for *ploce* above, or again with Richmond's reflections on Hope:

Kings it makes gods, and meaner creatures kings.   (v, ii, 24)

A related figure is *anadiplosis*, which gives the same word the last position in one clause and the first (or near the first) in the clause following. It rightly expresses causation, as in Richard's impatience:

Come, I have learn'd that fearful commenting
Is leaden servitor to dull delay;
Delay leads impotent and snail-pac'd beggary.   (IV, iii, 51–3)

If *anadiplosis* is carried through three or more clauses, it became a figure known in Greek as *climax* ('a ladder'; in Latin *gradatio*), and is again suitably used for causation in Richard's despair:

My conscience hath a thousand several tongues,
And every tongue brings in a several tale,
And every tale condemns me for a villain.   (v, iii, 193–5)

A more cutting type of repetition is the figure *polyptoton*, which takes a word and echoes it with another word derived from the same root:

Thou bloodless remnant of that royal blood!   (I, ii, 7)

This figure is sometimes said to be a pun, and can be grouped with the four main types of pun distinguished by rhetoric: *paronomasia* repeats a word similar in sound to one already used (and in its mature applications with an ironic distinction of sense):

> Not my deserts, but what I will deserve.   (IV, iv, 415)

or – a favourite Elizabethan pun, this –

> Cousins, indeed; and by their uncle cozen'd.   (IV, iv, 222)

Antanaclasis has a similar effect, in that it repeats a word while shifting from one meaning to another, as in Anne's curse on Richard for having killed her husband:

> O, cursed be the hand that made these holes!
> Cursed the heart that had the heart to do it!
> Cursed the blood that let his blood from hence!   (I, ii, 13–5)

By contrast *syllepsis* uses a word having two different meanings, without repeating it (an 'ambiguity', in modern terms), as when Richard promises Clarence 'your imprisonment shall not be long; / I will deliver or else lie for you' (I, i, 115), where 'lie' means (a) go to prison or (b) tell lies about. This is an especially apt figure for the double-faced Richard, and Shakespeare makes him comment on the fact:

> Thus, like the formal vice, Iniquity,
> I moralize two meanings in one word.   (III, i, 82–3)

The last type of pun is *asteismus*, particularly useful in drama, in which a word is returned by the answerer with an unlooked-for second meaning, as when Gloucester converts Brakenbury's defence into a bawdy joke.

> – With this, my lord, myself have nought to do.
> – Nought to do with Mistress Shore! I tell thee, fellow,
> He that doth nought with her, excepting one,
> Were best to do it secretly alone.   (I, i, 97–100)

or in Gloucester's later outrageous pun on 'Humphrey Hour' (IV, iv, 175). There is no need to illustrate a group of figures which are in general circulation: *zeugma* (the same verb for two disparate objects), *periphrasis, ellipsis, apostrophe*. If one reader's experience may be trusted to begin with, I would think that the figures listed here would provide the minimum necessary technical knowledge for an appreciation of a great deal of rhetorical usage.

But I am conscious that some readers may have another objection to the figures which I must briefly deal with before coming to discuss Shakespeare's developing use of rhetoric in prose and verse. The objection has indeed been made even by historians of rhetoric and scholars who have helped to reclaim other aspects of rhetoric for serious humane literary study, the objection that the figures are mere toys, 'husks', 'dry formulae', sterile patterns with no imaginative function. This is still the most serious objection to rhetoric, and if it were true then two thousand years of teaching and writing were disastrously wasted. But in fact rhetoricians of Greece, Rome and Renaissance England all argued that the figures had definite emotional and intellectual effects (see Vickers, 1970, ch. 3, for a fuller account). Rhetorical figures were conventions which had an important rationale, for theory held that by using them writers could best express feeling, could express it most naturally. This is an essential point to grasp, and if the illustration of it must be limited to the rhetoricians who were Shakespeare's contemporaries the functional nature of the figures will nevertheless be seen clearly.

Thus for the enlarged (1593) edition of his *Garden of Eloquence* (1577) Henry Peacham added a section on each figure giving 'The Use' and 'The Caution', stressing the need for the rhetorical device to be related to the sense and not to be over-used. So he urges that in figures like *anaphora, epanalepsis, ploce* and *epistrophe* the word chosen for repetition must be one vital to the sense (e.g. *epistrophe* 'serveth to leave a word of importance in the end of a sentence, that it may the longer hold the sound in the mind of the hearer', p. 43). Peacham picks out the 'figures of sentence' as being 'very sharp and vehement' (pp. 61–2) and says that such figures 'do attend upon affections (i.e. the passions), as ready handmaids at commandment to express most aptly whatsoever the heart doth affect or suffer' (p. 120): rhetoric re-enacts feeling. In his brief but intelligent *Directions for Speech and Style* (c. 1599), John Hoskins accepts that the word repeated be an important one, but seeks a psychological explanation for it: 'as no man is sick in thought upon one thing but for some vehemency or distress, so in speech there is no repetition without importance' (p. 12). Like all rhetoricians he holds that the figures not only re-create feeling in the character or action portrayed but therefore directly affect the feeling of the reader or playgoer: *anaphora* 'beats upon one thing to cause the quicker feeling in the audience' (p. 13). Like Peacham he urges the writer to tie the figure to sense and structure (the use of a figure should 'come from some choice and not from barrenness', p. 17), especially having regard to the organic needs of the whole: 'In these two sorts of amplifying you may insert all figures *'as the passion of the matter shall serve'*; *polyptoton* 'is a good figure, and may be used *with or without passion*' (pp. 21, 17; my italics). Finally, an equally sharp awareness of decorum and of the functional nature of the figures is shown by Puttenham in his *Arte of English Poesie* (1589). For Puttenham, as for many Renaissance men, the figures are essential to literature: 'the chief praise and cunning of our Poet is in the discreet using of his figures' (p. 138) (without them language is 'but as our ordinary talk'), yet they must be organically related to sense and feeling, and not extraneous, as in such clumsy repetitions as

'To love him and love him, as sinners should do.' These repetitions be not figurative but fantastical, for a figure is ever used to a purpose, either of beauty or of efficacy...(p. 202)

Elsewhere he shows what varied functions can be obtained by using *aposiopesis* (pp. 116–17), and reveals a remarkable awareness of the relationship between sound and sense in poetry (p. 196: on 'figures of sentence'). He concludes his account, as I mine, by pointing to the relationship between rhetoric and reality, Art and Nature: we all use rhetorical figures 'by very nature, without discipline' (teaching) according to our individual personalities, and rhetoric exists to refine and intensify their effect. 'Nature herself suggesteth the figure in this or that form: but Art aideth the judgment of his use and application' (p. 298). Rhetoric is not simply an imitation of nature, but almost a re-creation of it, in its own terms: 'rather a repetition or reminiscence natural, reduced into perfection, and made prompt by use and exercise' (p. 306).

I have cited some of the evidence from Renaissance rhetoricians here, despite the limitations of space, because for so long the historians and specialists in rhetoric have rejected the figures as irrelevant. This essay can only provide an outline of its subject, and it is for that reason especially important to establish an enlightened and humane attitude to the rhetorical figures, for without this further detailed work on rhetoric could not take place with any conviction of its literary validity. Shakespeare, like Puttenham or Longinus, evidently regarded the figures of rhetoric as having each their own range of relevance to states of mind or feeling. Rather than 'dry formulae' they are channels for feeling, pockets of energy, powerful and flexible according to the mind using them.

III

In his use of rhetoric as in other ways Shakespeare developed from stiffness to flexibility. He does not move away from rhetoric, rather he absorbs it into the tissue of living dramatic speech until it re-creates thought and feeling with a freshness which conceals its art. It is sometimes thought that there is less rhetoric in the later plays, but although we do not yet have an exhaustive study of his rhetorical development it seems to me unlikely that this is so. One can already see that of the many rhetorical figures in Shakespeare quoted by Sister Joseph the majority come from the mature plays, and this is not surprising, for it means that – as one might expect – Shakespeare only gradually learned to use the full resources of rhetoric. The same is true within Milton's development, for rhetoric only comes into its own in *Paradise Lost* (the early poems show a mastery of metaphor but not of the more expressive figures), and this points to a further truth in Shakespeare, that rhetoric is only stretched to its fullest when the action and characters themselves are of a depth and force to draw on the whole resources of language. J. M. Manly's early study of Chaucer's rhetoric was prepared to find the figures used frequently but did not expect to find them in the greatest poetry: 'that some of Chaucer's freest and most delightful work should contain twice as much rhetoric as some of his least inspired compositions is a puzzle that demands investigation.' It is not a puzzle: once we have grasped the functional potential of rhetoric it is self-evident that the greatest poetry may have often been based on the greatest use of rhetoric.

It would take many years to study Shakespeare's stylistic development with the attention it deserves, but a few examples can be given here, drawing by comparison on some of the figures already cited (I need hardly add that the discussion of individual figures taken out of their dramatic context is a crude and preliminary stage; the challenge facing students of rhetoric is to integrate the appreciation of stylistic detail into a response to the whole). One might juxtapose the rather stiff uses of rhetorical symmetry quoted from *Richard III* with a few lines in *Othello* which also combine *anaphora, isocolon, parison* and *epistrophe*, but to show Othello's trapped mind:

> By the world,
> I think my wife be honest, and think she is not;
> I think that thou art just, and think thou art not.
> I'll have some proof.   (III, iii, 388–90)

An external analysis would record that the same figures are used here as earlier, but evidently they now contain a much more intense and a much more personal kind of feeling, a feeling which is controlled by the symmetry because it is trapped by the action at this point. With the two correct but stiff uses of *gradatio* by Richard compare Othello's:

> No, Iago;
> I'll see before I doubt; when I doubt, prove;
> And, on the proof, there is no more but this –
> Away at once with love or jealousy!   (III, iii, 193–6)

Now the figure is again used for causation but it also expresses a whole view of life, that absolutist tendency in Othello to move to extremes once he is given an 'acceptable' basis which Iago can exploit to the full. And when it reaches its climax, the figure *antanaclasis* (repeating a word or phrase with a shift of meaning) has an incomparably sad and sinister effect:

> Put out the light, and then put out the light.   (v, ii, 7)

As the realization of his act begins to break through, Othello's awareness is rightly conveyed with *ploce* on the key word:

> If she come in she'll sure speak to my wife.
> My wife! my wife! what wife? I have no wife. (v, ii, 99–100)

And having punished himself Othello's dying words fall into the mould of *antimetabole*, without any sense of unnaturalness:

> I kiss'd thee ere I kill'd thee. No way but this –
> Killing my self, to die upon a kiss.   (v, ii, 361–2)

Such a brief juxtaposition of early and late is unsatisfactory as it necessarily fragments, but if taken further it could provide rewarding insights into Shakespeare's realization of the potential expressiveness of particular figures.

The more important task is to evaluate the development of his rhetoric within prose and verse, considering the whole dramatic context. I have elsewhere attempted such an analysis for the prose (Vickers, 1968), and I shall not duplicate my findings here. One important general point, though, which has bearings on Shakespeare's over-all development and on the problems of studying rhetoric in his poetry, is that I showed that his development in prose was not towards either a less extended use of rhetorical figures or a more speedy and brilliant interplay between diverse schemes, but rather that he continued to use the central corpus of figures to create passages of prose which are structurally similar but have an almost infinite range of dramatic functions. That is to say that if one rearranges the many rhetorical prose-speeches into their basic patterns the shape on the page is not fundamentally different between a Dromio and a Timon of Athens: both use *anaphora, parison, isocolon, epistrophe, antimetabole,* and so on. But the function of symmetry as a stress device within the stylistic and dramatic pattern of the play as a whole varies enormously. In the early clowns the speeches are basically catalogues of ridiculous behaviour, but the 'catalogue' later serves both as a satirical description of Ajax (limited in reference but dramatically organic), and for those extraordinary speeches of Poor Tom which refract so much of the

'Reason-in-Madness' of the later stages in *King Lear*. Proficiency in rhetoric can show the excellence of a character, whether for Henry V arguing with his soldiers on the eve of Agincourt and wooing Kate after the battle, or for the matching brilliance of Touchstone and Rosalind; but a fondness for symmetry can also show up the pomposity of Armado, the unsuitably formal political rhetoric of Brutus, and the varying degrees of frankness and deception within Falstaff. Rhetorical symmetry in prose is a tool for which Shakespeare found endless and unpredictable uses.

I would imagine that a chronological study of the development of his verse-rhetoric would reveal an analogous flexibility of reference, and although I do not have room to attempt it here a few points can be made. In the early work one will not be surprised to find that, as rhetoric had been the basis of both prose and verse since Gorgias, Shakespeare applies it to both media with equal stiffness and formality, so that the specific resources of verse tend to get swallowed up by the dominance of rhetorical patterning. Compare these two passages from *The Comedy of Errors*: first, Dromio of Ephesus complaining at the way his master treats him:

> When I am cold he heats me with beating;
> when I am warm he cools me with beating.
> I am wak'd with it when I sleep
> rais'd with it when I sit;
> driven out of doors with it when I go from home;
> welcom'd home with it when I return... (IV, iv, 29 ff)

Secondly, Adriana complaining that Antipholus neglects her:

> The time was once when thou unurg'd wouldst vow
> That never words were music to thine ear,
> That never object pleasing in thine eye,
> That never touch well welcome to thy hand,
> That never meat sweet-savour'd in thy taste,
> Unless I spake, or look'd or touch'd, or carv'd to thee.
> (II, ii, 112 ff)

Of course, the moods are widely different, but if anything the prose passage shows more inventiveness because it is free from the oppressive regularity of the decasyllabic line, which at this stage Shakespeare is using like building-bricks. (Study of his verse-rhetoric must be combined with that of all the other facets of verse – rhyme, metrics, use of varying line-lengths).

The nature of the development of his verse-rhetoric can be hinted at by the juxtaposition of early and late styles, this time in longer excerpts, relying on the reader's knowledge of the dramatic context.

First a part of the impassioned speech by Queen Margaret to Queen Elizabeth in *Richard III:*

> Where is thy husband now? Where be thy brothers?
> Where be thy two sons? Wherein dost thou joy?
> Who sues, and kneels, and says 'God save the Queen'?
> Where be the bending peers that flattered thee?
> Where be the thronging troops that followed thee?
> Decline all this, and see what now thou art:
> For happy wife, a most distressed widow;
> For joyful mother, one that wails the name;
> For one being su'd to, one that humbly sues;
> For Queen, a very caitiff crown'd with care;
> For she that scorn'd at me, now scorn'd of me;
> For she being fear'd of all now fearing one;
> For she commanding all, obey'd of none.   (IV, iv, 92–104)

The figures are so obvious that one hardly need name them – two long stretches of *anaphora*; *epistrophe* between lines ('thee' – 'thee') or within them ('at me' – 'of me'); *isocolon* and *parison* throughout, sometimes inventively (e.g. in line 3 the parallel verbs imitate the physical movement – 'sues' – 'kneels' – 'says'); *polyptoton* to help point up the ironic reversal of fortune ('su'd' – 'sues'; 'fear'd' – 'fearing'); *ploce* likewise ('scorn'd' – 'scorn'd'), and two witty uses of antithesis in the last two lines (especially the surprise echo to 'fear'd of all': 'now fearing one', i.e. Richard). It is a vigorous, dramatic speech which still makes its effect in the theatre, and rhetoric is certainly closely associated with feeling. But it is stiff, static, or in the more specific terms of this discussion, Shakespeare is manipulating the feeling *via* the rhetoric, from the outside. Nature has not yet digested the Art.

By contrast, as a parallel example at a similar level of mental excitement we might consider one of Leontes' speeches from *The Winter's Tale*. He is attacking Camillo, who has been trying to assure him that his 'diseas'd opinion' is groundless. Earlier in this tremendous scene Leontes' jealousy has been expressed in the most sinister word-play, as he teased unlooked for meanings out of words to convince himself that there had been a similar doubleness in deeds. But now the structural figures take over, as Leontes attacks with a devastating series of questions, the pressure being increased by *parison* linking the clauses together in a fixed mould, while the verbs are placed savagely at the beginning of each clause and in the form closest to action, *'doing'*:

> Is whispering nothing?
> Is leaning cheek to cheek? Is meeting noses?
> Kissing with inside lip? Stopping the career

Of laughter with a sigh? – a note infallible
Of breaking honesty. Horsing foot on foot?
Skulking in corners? Wishing clocks more swift;
Hours, minutes; noon, midnight?

The symmetry, the very structure of the verse shows the progressive breakdown of Leontes' mind; he is increasingly obsessed with the act, with what they might have done together (despite the confident-sounding questions he has no evidence – each is a figment of his imagination, given a definite-seeming status by the syntactical structure). The fast growth of the obsession is wonderfully conveyed by the figure *zeugma*, one verb doing duty for several objects, so speeding up the clock and the adulterers' imputed impatience: 'Wishing... Hours, minutes; noon, midnight', from the communal time to the time for private assignation.

Now to convince himself finally Leontes presents them deceiving everyone, with an effective use of *anadiplosis* ('but theirs, theirs only'):

And all eyes
Blind with the pin and web but theirs, theirs only,
That would unseen be wicked.

So far, from the first sentence onwards at the end of each question has been suspended the word 'nothing' (the parisonic structure makes it evident that this is understood at the end of each clause): 'Is whispering nothing?/Is leaning cheek to cheek [nothing]? Is meeting noses [nothing]?' Having been held in reserve for so long the word finally comes bursting out, with a quite devastating use of *epistrophe*:

– is this nothing?
Why, then the world and all that's in't is nothing;
The covering sky is nothing; Bohemia nothing;
My wife is nothing; nor nothing have these nothings,
If this be nothing.   (I, ii, 284–96)

In the penultimate clause indeed the word forces its way into the language before its time (*ploce*). We recall Peacham's caveat that the function of *epistrophe* is 'to leave a word of importance in the end of a sentence, that it may the longer hold the sound in the mind of the hearer', or better still John Hoskins' account of linguistic obsession: 'as no man is sick in thought upon one thing but for some vehemency or distress, so in speech there is no repetition without importance.' Both points are validated here, and there is a further irony that the 'word of importance' should be 'nothing', for indeed the answer to Leontes' questions is 'Yes, they are all nothing.' But for him it is a searing progression of certainties, and rhetoric channels it through

96

the figures. Here Shakespeare is experiencing the feeling from the inside, his intuitive grasp of human experience finding apparently natural outlet in the shapes of rhetoric.

Finally another example of verse-rhetoric from this play but in a very different mood, to show the variety of which the figures are capable when used creatively. In the sheep-shearing scene, at the end of the great flower-speech, Perdita regrets not having 'flow'rs o'th' spring' for the young, unmarried people, especially for Florizel 'To strew him o'er and o'er!' He protests at this passive role prescribed for him – 'What, like a corse?' – and Perdita denies it:

> No, like a bank for love to lie and play on;
> Not like a corse; or if – not to be buried,
> But quick, and in mine arms.

Already we see how rhetoric (*anaphora, parison*) can be used as a formal device to contain the fluid life of feeling, but in Florizel's response rhetoric both contains and displays his feeling and her unique and endless delight:

> What you do
> Still betters what is done. When you speak, sweet,
> I'd have you do it ever. When you sing,
> I'd have you buy and sell so; so give alms,
> Pray so; and, for the ord'ring your affairs,
> To sing them too. When you do dance, I wish you
> A wave o'th'sea, that you might ever do
> Nothing but that; move still, still so,
> And own no other function. Each your doing,
> So singular in each particular,
> Crowns what you are doing in the present deeds,
> That all your acts are queens. (IV, iv, 134–46)

To anyone with even a smattering of rhetoric it will be evident that much of what modern critics describe as the 'texture' of verse is in fact the product of a skilful use of rhetoric – density, smoothness, recurrence, fluidity. Here are many of the most formal schemes of rhetoric; three sentences are exactly symmetrical in structure ('When you speak...When you sing...When you do dance') but *anaphora*, *parison*, and *isocolon* perfectly convey Florizel's awe at her perfection in all her doings. 'Her doings' is the theme of the whole speech, so it is only right that *ploce* should put constant stress on 'you', and that *ploce* and *polyptoton* should wring every variant from the key verb, 'do': 'do, done, do, do, doing, doing, deeds' until she is crowned: 'all your acts are queens.' Other figures express the perfection of Perdita as she is: *anadiplosis* links together 'sell so; so give alms', or if we take it into the next line 'so' also ends that clause (*epanalepsis*).

At the comparison of Perdita to a wave, the verse takes on a wave-like motion, as several critics have noted, but it does so largely through rhetoric, by the cyclic repetition of 'you' and 'do', and again by *anadiplosis*: 'move still, still so.' And the figures are subtly played off against the verse-movement, with the symmetry now corresponding (lines 2–4), now diverging, using the line-division to accentuate the break within a symmetry (lines 4–5, 7–8). Here the mature Shakespearian style absorbs the structures of rhetoric to produce new and expressive structures of feeling. The early poetry displays its rhetoric stiffly, the mature style absorbs it: therefore modern criticism has been able to ignore the rhetorical framework in the mature style and discuss the life and feeling direct. But it seems at least likely that an awareness of the forms of rhetoric can enlarge our understanding of the poetry, for in Shakespeare's time and in Shakespeare's poetry rhetoric and feeling were one.

7

SHAKESPEARE'S POETRY

INGA-STINA EWBANK

Nature her selfe was proud of his designes,
  And ioy'd to weare the dressing of his lines!
Which were so richly spun, and wouen so fit,
  As, since, she will vouchsafe no other Wit.

Ben Jonson, 'To the Memory of...Mr. William Shakespeare'
(1623)

We should expect a dramatic poet like Shakespeare to write his finest poetry
in his most dramatic scenes. And this is just what we do find...The same
plays are the most poetic and the most dramatic, and this not by a con-
currence of two activities, but by the full expansion of one and the same
activity.   T. S. Eliot, 'A Dialogue on Dramatic Poetry' (1928)

I

Three hundred years separate Ben Jonson's and T. S. Eliot's statements, but they are united in their assurance that Shakespeare's poetry
was above all a superb means of dramatic expression. Eliot had to
rediscover what Jonson could take for granted: that in Shakespeare the
Poet and the Dramatist were, like the Phoenix and Turtle in his own
poem, 'single nature's double name'. This is of course only one out
of a multitude of possible ways of talking about Shakespeare's poetry.
I have chosen it because I believe it to be the most important way, and
also because it is impossible in a single essay to deal fully with even
a single aspect of Shakespeare's poetry – let alone with them all. One
might attempt to give an account of the wide range and scope of his
verse as well as its fine nuances and precise and evocative details; of
the way his rhythms and imagery altered as he gained ever-greater
control of his medium; of his sense of decorum, in the widest application of the word, which means that each of his works has its own poetic
qualities and raises its own problems. But to do this – to face all these
and many more issues, all of them interrelated – would, as in Milton's
poem 'On Shakespeare', tend to 'make *us* marble with too much
conceiving'. The reader must regard this essay as an introduction to
the dramatic poet rather than an exhaustive examination of Shakespeare's poetry.

99

Eliot's view of the poet and dramatist as 'two distincts, division none' heralds, in time if not in fact, the generation of scholars and critics to whom present-day students of Shakespeare owe so much. Critics like G. Wilson Knight, Caroline Spurgeon and Wolfgang Clemen – to mention only the pioneers – have taught us to see Shakespeare's poetry as integral to his dramatic fabric. At worst, and in the wrong hands, the approach to each Shakespeare work as 'an expanded metaphor' (G. Wilson Knight) has meant undue concentration on the verse alone, or on iterative imagery, or on Shakespeare's verbal symbolism as a sort of quasi-philosophical system. At best it has meant seeing the poems – especially the sonnets – and the plays as products of the same imaginative process.

Shakespeare himself was reticent about the nature of that process. No doubt most of us feel that he, if anyone, justifies Coleridge's exalted definition of the 'primary Imagination' as 'a repetition in the finite mind of the eternal act of creation in the infinite I AM'; but the nearest he gets to the description of such a creative act is in Theseus' account of how

> The poet's eye, in a fine frenzy rolling,
> Doth glance from heaven to earth, from earth to heaven;
> And as imagination bodies forth
> The forms of things unknown, the poet's pen
> Turns them to shapes, and gives to airy nothing
> A local habitation and a name.
> (*A Midsummer Night's Dream* v, i, 12–17)

And in the dramatic context Theseus is dismissive, even derisive, of the Romantic visionary, placing the poet with the lunatic and the lover as men 'of imagination all compact'. Closer to the Renaissance ideal of the poet as an eloquent teacher is the Poet in *Timon of Athens*, who is also given finer lines about the nature of poetic inspiration –

> our gentle flame
> Provokes itself, and like the current flies
> Each bound it chafes – (i, i, 25–7)

than his opportunist approach to writing, as demonstrated in the play, deserves. But the limitations of a view of poetry as the art of giving outward form to an inner moral are exposed when the Painter tells the Poet:

> A thousand moral paintings I can show
> That shall demonstrate these quick blows of Fortune's
> More pregnantly than words. (i, i, 93–5)

Shakespeare's whole corpus testifies to the fact that he believed in the pregnancy of words over 'a thousand moral paintings', in the power of imaginative poetry to reach further than any merely visual image. Hamlet, for one, expresses this belief when he rebukes his mother,

> 'Tis not alone my inky cloak, good mother,
>
> ....
>
> That can denote me truly...
>
> ....
>
> But I have that within which passes show –
> These but the trappings and the suits of woe,
>
> (*Hamlet* I, ii, 77–86)

and then proceeds, through the rest of the play, to use all the resources of language to demonstrate 'that within'.

Unlike his fellow-sonneteer Sidney, Shakespeare left no Apology for Poetry; unlike such of his fellow-dramatists as Nashe, Greene, Jonson, Chapman or Webster, he left no comments outside his plays on what he thought good drama and good poetry should be like. From the plays we can learn something of what he thought they should *not* be like. Mocking of 'taffeta phrases, silken terms precise, / Three-piled hyperboles, spruce affectation, / Figures pedantical' plays a large part in *Love's Labour's Lost*, and most of the other love comedies contain references to literary affectations and mannerisms. Not many agree that *Titus Andronicus* is a parody on 'the height of Seneca his style' as practised by the tragic dramatists of the late 1580s and the early 90s, but the verse of the Mousetrap in *Hamlet* certainly is; and the 'very tragical mirth' of the Pyramus and Thisbe interlude in *A Midsummer Night's Dream* takes off the cruder forms of contemporary dramatic and non-dramatic literature – even, some would say, Shakespeare's own *Romeo and Juliet*. But in none of these cases is the literary satire the main point: it is part of and subordinated to a dramatic exploration of the false as against the genuine, fiction as against reality. Deliberately 'bad' Shakespearean poetry is sometimes functional *rather than* parodic. The nurse's mock-Senecan fulminations against the 'woeful, woeful, woeful day' in *Romeo and Juliet* IV, v, serve to set Juliet's mock-death here off from her real one in the last scene. Othello's departure from his real self, at the point where he definitely succumbs to Iago's persuasions, is measured by his assumption of the voice of the conventional Revenger:

> Arise, black vengeance, from the hollow hell.
> Yield up, O love, thy crown and hearted throne
> To tyrannous hate! Swell, bosom...
>
> (*Othello* III, iii, 451–3)

If the 'poetic' of the plays is often negatively stated and always embodied in the dramatic whole, the sonnets more clearly show

Shakespeare reflecting on his own poetic practice and comparing it with that of others. For example, Shakespeare refuses to 'glance aside / To new-found methods, and to compounds strange' (76), and he has ambivalent feelings about 'the proud full sail' of the Rival Poet's 'great verse' (86). As Joan Grundy has pointed out, Shakespeare and Sidney alone among Elizabethan sonneteers question the aims and methods of the Petrarchan convention which they inherited. But Shakespeare's, unlike Sidney's, questioning is not so much a literary quarrel as part of a larger concern with rendering the real image of the person he is writing of and to and for – the Youth (1–126) and the Dark Lady (127–152). His poet's prayer is: 'O, let me, true in love, but truly write' (21); and to write truly means to show 'that you alone are you' (84). Even in the best-known piece of mockery of Petrarchan love-poetry, 'My mistress' eyes are nothing like the sun' (130), the mockery itself is the staircase by which we climb to the real point of the poem, the celebration of the 'rareness' of the Lady:

> And yet, by heaven, I think my love as rare
> As any she belied with false compare.

Explicitly, then, in the sonnets, Shakespeare is striving for a subordination of the style to the subject matter. Ideally, the style *is* the subject:

> O, know, sweet love, I always write of you,
> And you and love are still my argument;   (76)

> In others' works thou dost but mend the style,
> And arts with thy sweet graces graced be;
> But thou art all my art.   (78)

That this is not merely an echo of Sidney's 'Look in thy heart and write', but is meant as well as said, is shown by the texture and structure of the individual sonnets. Whatever the 'true' facts behind the 1609 volume of *Sonnets* – and this is not the place to enter into the controversy about the identities of Mr W.H., the Fair Youth, the Rival Poet and the Dark Lady – it remains a poetically true record of two different love relationships, with the fluctuations of mind and mood involved in each. In the first 126 sonnets the Youth is re-created, not in static perfection but dramatically pitted against the enemies that threaten: the flatterers without, his own unfaithfulness within and – all around – the very condition of man as he is subjected to inexorable Time. The greater the threat, the keener the imaginative realization of the enemy's attack and the poet's counter-attack:

> Like as the waves make towards the pebbled shore,
> So do our minutes hasten to their end;
> Each changing place with that which goes before,

In sequent toil all forwards do contend.
Nativity, once in the main of light,
Crawls to maturity, wherewith being crown'd,
Crooked eclipses 'gainst his glory fight,
And Time that gave doth now his gift confound.
Time doth transfix the flourish set on youth,
And delves the parallels in beauty's brow,
Feeds on the rarities of nature's truth,
And nothing stands but for his scythe to mow.
 And yet to times in hope my verse shall stand,
 Praising thy worth, despite his cruel hand.   (60)

J. W. Lever, in a particularly fine analysis of this sonnet, has shown how it 'achieves its own poetic miracle by taking an entire chain of images from the speech of Ovid's Pythagoras [in the *Metamorphoses*] and fusing them at white heat with the themes of the sonnet sequence'. In sonnets like this we have the implicit application of Shakespeare's explicit poetic. But we have it in lesser sonnets, too. Even in the lines which I quoted from Sonnet 78, the style embodies the meaning. The pretty pattern of sound and sense in 'arts with thy sweet graces graced be' resolves itself into the monosyllabic plainness of 'but thou art all my art', where yet the crucial pun on 'art' shows that the plainness is carefully controlled artifice. It is artifice of a lower imaginative order than that behind the careful structuring of evocative images in Sonnet 60; but in neither poem does the style simply illustrate or decorate a thought. The greatest sonnets, whether to the Youth or to the Lady, *enact* the impact of the beloved on the poet, through their diction, their imagery, their rhythm and their structural pattern – whether it be the rise from despondency to jubilation through 'thy sweet love rememb'red' in Sonnet 29, or the downward movement to the realization that 'Time will come and take my love away' of sonnet 64, or the tug-of-war impulses of 'Th'expense of spirit in a waste of shame' in Sonnet 129.

Already we have seen that when Shakespeare sets about applying his sonnet poetic – the fusion of subject and style, matter and manner – this involves qualities which are dramatic as well as poetic. It involves the arrangement of words and images into a pattern which is formal, not merely in the external sense that it consists of three quatrains and a clinching couplet, but in the sense that it imitates an action. And it involves the rendering of the general through the particular, so that the beloved's image, 'most rich in youth', is part of the consciousness that 'every thing that grows / Holds in perfection but a little moment' (15). Both these are essential, and common, to all great dramatists. But there is also another, perhaps peculiarly Shakespearean, quality involved. Read as a whole, the *Sonnets* show an apparently paradoxical combination of a tremendous interest in words and belief in their power with a kind of humbleness about the possibilities of language.

The very desire to show 'that you alone are you' makes the poet conscious of the inadequacy of poetry:

> Who will believe my verse in time to come,
> ....
> If I could write the beauty of your eyes
> And in fresh numbers number all your graces,
> The age to come would say 'This poet lies;
> Such heavenly touches ne'er touch'd earthly faces.'
> So should my papers, yellowed with their age,
> Be scorn'd, like old men of less truth than tongue. (17)

The truth-tongue opposition in that last line reminds us of a key *motif* in *Richard II*. Richard D. Altick, in an important study of 'symphonic imagery' in this play, shows how

that words are mere conventional sounds molded by the tongue, and reality is something else again, is constantly on the minds of all the characters.

Most critics agree that *Richard II* is a milestone in Shakespeare's poetic–dramatic development, and that the play – like its poet-hero – is uniquely self-conscious about the power *and* limitations of language. But the sonnets' questioning of language reverberates right through to the end of Shakespeare's career. In Sonnet 23, the intensity of the poet's emotion outruns words altogether:

> O, let my looks be then the eloquence
> And dumb presagers of my speaking breast;
> Who plead for love, and look for recompense,
> More than that tongue that more hath more express'd.
> O learn to read what silent love hath writ!
> To hear with eyes belongs to love's fine wit.

Shakespeare is here talking about what in *The Winter's Tale* he puts into a stage-image, when he makes the reunion of Leontes and Hermione wordless. In that scene he shows his awareness, as a dramatist, of realities which language cannot get at, not even the subtle tool of his own poetry.

Part of Shakespeare's poetic belief is that what *is* cannot always be said. In this context one should mention his enigmatic poem *The Phoenix and Turtle* – his contribution to the miscellany called *Loves Martyr* (1601) – for it represents his furthest reaching out in words towards what cannot be articulated. It is an incantatory celebration of a love so great and pure and mysterious as to be able to transcend nature and reason, and it is in that sense an extension, in one particular direction, of the sonnets as well as an anticipation of central themes in the Romances. But in its structure and handling of language it strangely anticipates the dramatic rhythm of the closing scenes of *King Lear*, from IV, vi, onwards. The death and victory of Phoenix and the turtle is represented through the 'anthem' of the mourning birds and the 'threnos' spoken by Reason:

> Beauty, truth, and rarity,
> Grace in all simplicity,
> Here enclos'd in cinders lie.
> ....
> Truth may seem, but cannot be;
> Beauty brag, but 'tis not she:
> Truth and beauty buried be.

So at the height of his agony – albeit this is suffering and victory of a different kind – Lear is surrounded by characters who sympathetically participate in what they cannot fully comprehend. There, too, we have statements of utter simplicity in the face of the unbearable, the too great, too complex; and that simplicity has, as in the poem, a kind of imperious finality, as in Edgar's aside at IV, vi, 141–2:

> I would not take this from report. It is,
> And my heart breaks at it.

As in the poem, whatever the central action means, '*it is*'; and all that the survivors can ultimately say is that 'we that are young / Shall never see so much nor live so long'.

The Phoenix and Turtle, because of its purity of diction and lyrical form, has often been compared to the songs in Shakespeare's plays, although of course it is much more intellectual and metaphysically complex than any of the songs. With the songs it also shares the quality of expressing through simple juxtaposition of images or statements, through the combination of words into an incantation rather than an argument, what more logically structured dramatic dialogue cannot express. Shakespeare's songs have increasingly been recognized as dramatically functional, and one of their functions – in the mature plays at least – is to say what could otherwise not be said in the plays where they occur. We need only think of Feste's concluding song which by illogic draws together the discordant elements in *Twelfth Night*; or Ophelia's mad songs; or Desdemona's willow-song, which is the only form in which she can articulate her sense of what is happening.

It would be very wrong to give the impression that Shakespeare, like some modern dramatists, was preoccupied with the non-meaning

of language and the impossibility of communication. The plays themselves, through to Prospero's eloquent farewell to his art, are evidence
enough to the contrary. Through the sonnets there surges a powerful
belief in his own verse, gathered into explicit assertion in the group
that deals with the immortalizing of the Friend by his poetry –
supremely in Sonnet 55:

> Not marble nor the gilded monuments
> Of princes shall outlive this pow'rful rhyme;
> But you shall shine more bright in these contents
> Than unswept stone, besmear'd with sluttish time.

In this sonnet he makes new a commonplace conceit which Renaissance poets took over from Ovid (thus proving his point by the very
writing of the poem). In other sonnets, such as 'Let me not to the
marriage of true minds / Admit impediments' (116), it is by the perfect
handling of some of the simplest words in the language that he makes
his assertion of belief both in his subject and in his poetry. The reason
why it is important to stress Shakespeare's sense (to us perhaps
unwarranted) of the limitations of his poetry is that it is part of the
poetic, in the deepest sense, of the sonnets and of the plays. The poetry
not the poet matters, and the poetry matters as the true image of its
subject. The reason why the sonnets are the greatest love poems in the
language is also the reason why Shakespeare is the greatest poetic
dramatist. We could call it selflessness – and critics have often drawn
attention to the lack of self-assertion in Shakespeare's sonnets, compared
to those of his contemporaries. We could borrow Keats's phrase and
call it 'negative capability'. In either case we are talking of the man
whose 'nature is subdu'd / To what it works in, like the dyer's hand'
(Sonnet 111). And perhaps that is the nearest we can get to a generalization about the poetic *and* dramatic 'activity' which T. S. Eliot spoke of.

II

In making this generalization one is of course cutting across all those
variations within sonnets and between sonnets, within plays and
between plays, that we usually sum up as Shakespeare's development.
How did Shakespeare find his own idiom?

Talking about 'development' within the sonnets is dangerous, for
it is unlikely that the scholarly debate about the dates of individual
sonnets, and about the time-limits within which the whole sequence
was written, will ever be settled. But, whatever their chronological
position (and one would like to think that they are apprentice work),
there are sonnets which do not rise above the level of the conventional

Petrarchan exercise, cleverly refurbishing old conceits and playing the fashionable game on the themes of sleeplessness, absence or the war between eye and heart. For extreme examples one may turn to Sonnets 153 and 154, the anticlimactic conclusion to the 1609 volume. They are variations on a theme borrowed from the *Greek Anthology*: a nymph steals the arrow of sleeping Cupid and quenches its 'love-kindling fire' in a cool well, which thus becomes

> a bath and healthful remedy
> For men diseas'd; but I, my mistress' thrall,
> Came there for cure, and this by that I prove:
> Love's fire heats water, water cools not love.   (154)

It is difficult to see anything 'Shakespearean' about this – and indeed Dover Wilson thought these two poems 'early essays, if indeed they are Shakespeare's at all'. What the poem is communicating is not so much the paradoxical impulses of a love relationship as the poet's pleasure at his own ingenuity: at the verbal pattern of the last line and the way this clinches, with a q.e.d. finality, the argument of the conceit. The poets of the 1590s were often intoxicated with word-patterns; and, unless this is a cynical exercise, Shakespeare, when he wrote it, had yet to learn how to make such patterns expressive rather than exhibitionist. (One might compare Peele's use of a similar patterning, on a similar subject, to make a sensuous and moving impact in the opening song of *David and Bethsabe*.)

But one does not have to read far to discover that Shakespeare could make verbal ingenuity a means of communicating a sense of life. Thus in this passage from a sonnet on an apparently conventional subject,

> When most I wink, then do mine eyes best see,
> For all the day they view things unrespected;
> But when I sleep, in dreams they look on thee,
> And, darkly bright, are bright in dark directed;
> Then thou whose shadow shadows doth make bright,
> How would thy shadow's form form happy show
> To the clear day with thy much clearer light,
> When to unseeing eyes thy shade shines so,   (43)

the style is not simply drawing attention to itself. The pattern of accumulating paradoxes and antitheses becomes an enactment of how the vision of the beloved gives new content to old words. The meaning of shadows and forms, brightness and darkness, is, as it were, revalued; until the dramatic sense of life deserves a comparison with the last line of Milton's sonnet on his deceased wife:

> I waked, she fled, and day brought back my night.

But where in Milton the reversal of meanings embodies personal tragedy, the mood evoked here is of joy; and G. K. Hunter has nicely described the line 'And, darkly bright, are bright in dark directed' as 'a triumphant dance of words expressing the lover's delight'.

In what we presume to be later sonnets, obvious artifice gives way to the kind of realism which consists in prosaic diction, 'unpoetical' imagery and a rhythm approaching that of the speaking voice. Shakespeare is reflecting, or anticipating, the general stylistic development that we tend to think of as a movement from an Elizabethan to a Jacobean mode of writing; and, in so doing, he is serving his own expressive needs. It is not a question of realistic writing in a modern sense. Sonnets 118 ('Like as to make our appetites more keen') and 147 ('My love is as a fever, longing still / For that which longer nurseth the disease') are as ingenious in their use of metaphor as are sonnets 153–4; but the artifice is now so carefully controlled as to give an impression of nature. While the Cupid-nymph-lover poems fail to communicate the torments of a love where one has 'garner'd up' one's heart, 118 and 147 render, respectively, the agonized experience of a beloved's unfaithfulness and the 'frantic mad' passion for a woman who, the poet *knows*, is 'as black as hell, as dark as night'. Word-patterns in sonnets like these take on a precision which, supported by the movement of the verse, follows the curve of feeling:

> Enjoy'd no sooner but despised straight;
> Past reason hunted, and, no sooner had,
> Past reason hated, ...
> ....
> Had, having, and in quest to have, extreme;
> A bliss in proof, and prov'd, a very woe.　　(129)

Shakespeare did more than any other sonneteer to enlarge the human content and expand the thematic range of the sonnet. Even so, the sonnets' scope for action and character is necessarily limited; and they can only give us an outline map of Shakespeare's development as a poetic dramatist. But if they show us Shakespeare moving from a kind of group style, characterized by rather self-conscious use of verbal artifice, through an individual use of elements of that group style, to an individual style in which artifice and nature are so blended that – in Polixenes' words – 'the art itself is nature'; then they also give us a paradigm – not of course to be used too rigidly – for the development of Shakespeare's dramatic poetry.

Elizabethan tragedy of the 1580s and 90s was trying to combine the epic structure of native drama with the unified form of Senecan tragedy in which the hero contemplates his suffering. The result, in terms of style, tends to be a language written for orators, to comment on tableaux, rather than for actors, to make particular dramatic situations and characters alive to the audience. Speeches are often structured on a rhetorical scheme, supported by heavy (and at worst mechanical) alliteration; the imagery tends towards self-conscious similes; the lines are stiffly end-stopped. The language tends to make the impression of having an action of its own, counterpointed to the human reality within the drama. Take, for example, the speech of the dying Mortimer in *1 Henry VI*:

> Even like a man new haled from the rack,
> So fare my limbs with long imprisonment;
> And these grey locks, the pursuivants of death,
> Nestor-like aged in an age of care,
> Argue the end of Edmund Mortimer.
> These eyes, like lamps whose wasting oil is spent,
> Wax dim, as drawing to their exigent;
> Weak shoulders, overborne with burdening grief,
> And pithless arms, like to a withered vine
> That droops his sapless branches to the ground.
> Yet are these feet, whose strengthless stay is numb,
> Unable to support this lump of clay,
> Swift-winged with desire to get a grave,
> As witting I no other comfort have.   (II, v, 3–16)

In its way, this is a moving speech, but it has to be a long one, for it can make its impact only by accretion. The Elizabethans were triumphantly aware of what Richard Carew, in *The Excellency of the English Tongue* (*c.* 1595), termed 'our tongue's copiousness' and particularly of its richness in 'fruitful and forcible' metaphors. Yet even when Mortimer has taken an inventory from his locks down to his feet, he has left us with a list of items which, however 'forcibly' each is illustrated, do not merge to prove an experience upon our pulses. The scheme of the speech is not so rigid as Hieronimo's notorious outburst of grief ('O eyes! no eyes, but fountains fraught with tears', *The Spanish Tragedy* III, ii, 1 ff), but it has the same basis in a linguistic, rather than experiential, pattern, pointed by alliteration, word-play ('aged in an age of care') and the accumulation of adjectives with similar endings ('pithless', 'sapless', 'strengthless'). We may compare this with the speech of another character who also feels that he belongs with the rack and the grave:

> You do me wrong to take me out o'th'grave.
> Thou art a soul in bliss; but I am bound
> Upon a wheel of fire, that mine own tears
> Do scald like molten lead.   (*King Lear* IV, vii, 45–8)

Lear needs four lines to communicate infinitely more than Mortimer in his fourteen, and the 'more' is to be measured not in quantity but in quality. Where Mortimer's poetry plays as a kind of decoration over the dramatic situation, Lear's *is* the situation, truly proving upon our pulses what this particular debilitated body feels like and what its spiritual condition is. The language is shaped by the structure of the human experience: literal and metaphorical levels have merged (Lear thinks he *is* in Purgatory, not that he is 'as if'), and the alliteration measures the gulf which he senses between himself and Cordelia ('Thou art a soul in *b*liss; *b*ut I am *b*ound...'). The single metaphor ('like molten lead'), which also contains the single adjective of the passage, renders the intensity, rather than the structure, of the experience. These features are related to the whole poetic quality of *King Lear*, brilliantly analysed by Winifred Nowottny, of being so concerned with simply underlining the intensity of suffering made manifest in the dramatic action that there is little need for analytical imagery to communicate 'what it feels like'. Stage-directions – like '*Enter* Lear, *with* Cordelia *dead in his arms*' – or references to what we can see for ourselves – like 'a head so old and white as this' – become more eloquent than similes or metaphors in a play which concludes on Edgar's exhortation to 'speak what we feel, not what we ought to say'. Mortimer remains articulate, indeed a very systematic chronicler of past history, to his end; and Richard Plantagenet's conventional epitaph on him turns his experience into a generalized allegory:

> And peace, no war, befall thy parting soul!
> In prison hast thou spent a pilgrimage,
> And like a hermit overpass'd thy days.
> (*1 Henry VI* II, v, 115–17)

Lear's dying moments are verbally as broken and tormented, torn to shreds between hope and despair, as the man himself; and as Kent speaks on his death, his words keep the attention riveted on Lear's specific agony:

> Vex not his ghost. O, let him pass! He hates him
> That would upon the rack of this tough world
> Stretch him out longer.   (v, iii, 313–15)

While we thus perceive Lear's individual fate more keenly than Mortimer's, we are yet at the same time more keenly aware of its universal dimension. This is very largely the achievement of the poetry, and partly of the imagery. In making Kent return to the image of the rack, Shakespeare not only reminds us of the earlier scene (IV, vii) but also introduces, in a climactic fashion, a *motif* dominant throughout the play. Ever since Miss Spurgeon's exposition of leading motives in the imagery of Shakespeare's plays, and since Professor Clemen's study of the *dramatic* function of imagery, we have been able to appreciate the way in which iterative imagery spreads a whole network of subterranean connections, often in defiance of ordinary logic, between passages, linking them structurally, fitting them into the whole imaginative fabric of the play, and so expanding issues that the play as a whole asks questions and makes statements larger than a mere plot-paraphrase would suggest. Every student now knows, for example, that disease and poison are dominant images in *Hamlet*; evil, darkness and babes in *Macbeth*; that cosmic and food imagery renders the polarity of *Antony and Cleopatra* – and, indeed, that *King Lear* is dominated by the image of 'a human body in anguished movement, tugged, wrenched, ...tortured and finally broken on the rack' (Miss Spurgeon). We can also now more readily appreciate the effect of recurring key-words – like 'see' in *King Lear* – which cumulatively gain the dramatic and thematic power of images.

But not only imagery links Kent's speech with the poetic and dramatic whole of *King Lear*. The very mode of his speech – his two initial exclamations and the aggressiveness of 'He hates him...' – is that predominant in the play as a whole. ('Blow, winds, and crack your cheeks; rage, blow.' 'Come not between the dragon and his wrath.') It has been pointed out how the plays of Shakespeare's maturity tend to have their typical speech-modes – the questions in *Hamlet*; the ambiguities and equivocations in *Macbeth*; and the exclamations and very simple but also very basic questions in *King Lear* – which not only set the mood for the play but express in epitome its spiritual core. The rhythm of Kent's speech is in itself so close to the speaking voice, and the syntax so expressive of the character Kent at this particular moment, that no superimposed art is apparent (or perhaps even conscious on the part of the author). But here is another way in which the single speech is subordinated to the over-all form of the play; and one is reminded of M. C. Bradbrook's description of 'the central core' of each Shakespeare play as 'an informing power radiating and glowing through every tissue and fibre of the whole, down to the single word'.

If, on the paradigm of Shakespeare's utilization of his poetic gifts, Lear's and Mortimer's speeches represent the two extremes of art and artifice, then the speeches of Richard II, and especially his prison speech in V, v, might represent a mid-way point. Here we have elaborate and self-conscious verbal artifice – extended metaphors, carefully balanced antitheses, intricate word-play – but here, too, the artifice reflects the very nature of the hero and of his tragic dilemma. He is a man who can control words, but not reality. Furthermore,

Shakespeare is not simply letting Richard indulge himself in verbal wit for the sake of character revelation. The speech contains the climactic occurrence of many key-words and image patterns which have been weaving through the play in a 'symphonic' fashion. Its poetry creates a structural as well as thematic resolution for the play as a whole. Guided by Richard Altick, to whose essay I have already referred, we may see *Richard II* as pointing the continuity between the exuberant and often uncontrolled word-play of Shakespeare's earlier plays and the highly controlled use of great image-themes in the plays of his mature period. Both characteristics testify to his associative poetic power; the difference between them testifies to his development from a dramatic poet to a poetic dramatist.

In concentrating on a few chosen passages, I have obviously begged many questions and excluded vast areas of Shakespearean dramatic verse. The qualities to be found in the *Henry VI* plays could, to a large extent, be paralleled in *Titus Andronicus*; but already *Romeo and Juliet* shows Shakespeare discovering new dramatic possibilities within contemporary poetic conventions – such as using a love sonnet for the dialogue of Romeo and Juliet's first meeting. The early, middle and 'Problem' comedies present their own features and problems, which the scope of this essay cannot hold. The poetry of *King Lear*, like that of all the great tragedies, is not typical of anything but itself. The longer and more analytical speeches of Hamlet or Macbeth would have provided better examples of Shakespeare making rhythm, diction and imagery expressive of a character's inner life, while also suggesting the general through the particular – so that in Macbeth's 'If it were done...' we both *know* his state of mind and sense something about good, evil and damnation in general. The poetry of the Roman plays, and especially of *Coriolanus* with its 'public' use of language and its deliberately non-evocative imagery, would have illustrated the shaping power of Shakespeare's sense of decorum. (Students of the Roman plays are indebted to Maurice Charney for his analysis of their style, or styles.) And, finally, the poetry of the Last Plays defies generalizations as much as that of the others, but in different ways. They contain passages as tense and expressive as anything in the tragedies (one thinks, for example, of Leontes's jealousy); but there are also passages that seem to return to an earlier, decorative or artificial mode. Granville-Barker even spoke of 'a new euphuism of imagination' in these plays. And there is, too, a new kind of elliptical writing which James Sutherland has discussed in a provocative essay. It is as if Shakespeare were at times forcing the situation to yield meanings which it can barely sustain, or as if the metaphysical mode were swamping the dramatic.

With all these qualifications made (and many not made that should have been), the passages on which I have been concentrating yield a few simple truths about Shakespeare's development. They show that it is a matter of the way language is subordinated to subject matter. The artistic growth here is obviously to be seen in terms of both language and subject. The *King Lear* passage is better than the one from *Henry VI* not simply because it contains better poetry – or, as Mrs Nowottny has put it,

With Shakespeare, the language that 'makes' the play depends in the first instance on his making the kind of play in which it is possible and proper to speak it.

What is involved, is an ever-growing sensitivity to language, inextricably tied up with an ever-larger sensitivity to human experience. That Shakespeare was interested in life can be proved (if it needs proving) from all his poetry: one could point to the almost obsessive urge in the sonnets to give the beloved life within the medium of language; or to the way abstracts come alive in his language; or one could simply refer to Miss Spurgeon. However much one doubts her biographical interpretation of Shakespeare's imagery – Shakespeare's feelings about dogs or the eddy under the Clopton bridge – one must believe her when she says that 'it is the life of things which appeals to him, stimulates and enchants him, rather than beauty of colour or form or even significance'. And clearly different aspects of life interested him more or differently at different times in his career. However mythical his sorrows, when he wrote *Troilus and Cressida* he needed, and found, a language for the violence of sex and the destructiveness of Time which he had not found when he wrote *The Two Gentlemen of Verona* and did not need when he wrote *The Winter's Tale*. It is the amount of felt life in his dramatic poetry which first and last moves us; and this is proved at the simplest level by the way our own experiences modify our reactions to his lines. It does not matter how many children Lady Macbeth had, but every woman who has nursed a baby will ever afterwards feel more strongly about her 'I have given suck' speech, as about Cleopatra's 'Dost thou not see my baby...'. At another level it is proved by the effect which his characters produce of being – in Eric Bentley's phrase – 'in the world'. Through the verse we perceive the dynamism of ideas passing in and out of their minds: Macbeth is probably the clearest example. We see their minds being coloured by an event or an idea (Hamlet), or even usurped by someone else's vision of life, as is the case with Othello in III, iii. We see the dialogue developing into a record of the interaction of minds, so that the last fifty-five lines of *Macbeth* I, vii, become a living image of how

Macbeth's will feeds upon Lady Macbeth's and is spurred by it, until he can speak the final couplet with what is virtually her voice. (Irving in fact gave the last two lines to Lady Macbeth, thus spoiling the point.) We see the formalized stichomythia of early tragedy translated into the head-on clash of alienated and opposed sensibilities –

QUEEN   Hamlet, thou hast thy father much offended.
HAMLET Mother, you have my father much offended.
QUEEN   Come, come, you answer with an idle tongue.
HAMLET Go, go, you question with a wicked tongue—
(*Hamlet* III, iv, 9–12)

or, at the opposite extreme, into the complete and sympathetic sharing of experience at the end of *King Lear*:

KENT   Is this the promis'd end?
EDGAR   Or image of that horror?
ALBANY Fall and cease!
(*King Lear* v, iii, 263–4)

There can hardly be a more obvious example in dramatic literature of the audience off and on stage participating in a moment of only-too-keenly felt life.

But no amount of felt life in single and separate moments will make a play. For the dynamic and sustained, and yet concentrated, rendering of life that is drama, there must be a coherent relationship between all the moments: a form. If one part of Shakespeare's unique gift is a genius for language that expresses human experience, the other part is a genius for form that organizes words and experience into an imaginative whole.

It may, finally, be a hallmark of his art that within each play this imaginative unity co-exists with a greater variety of styles than we find in any other major dramatist. In no play is that variety more striking, nor more functional, than in *Antony and Cleopatra*. It is a play where we are constantly being asked to move through dimensions: of time (the Antony that was *versus* the Antony that is), of space (Rome *versus* Egypt), and of language (the cosmic *versus* the human, the heroic *versus* the humorous, the superlative *versus* the very ordinary). Cleopatra's image has room for the barge-speech *and* for the nurse being sucked asleep by the babe at her breast; for 'Royal Egypt, Empress!' *and* for 'e'en a woman, and commanded / By such poor passion as the maid that milks / And does the meanest chares'. The play's poetry delights in defying expectations, using the simplest imagery at the most exalted moments. When Antony dies in Cleopatra's arms, what starts as a 'high' speech turns quietly towards a sense of personal loss and a feeling that:

> Young boys and girls
> Are level now with men. The odds is gone,
> And there is nothing left remarkable
> Beneath the visiting moon.   (IV, xv, 65–8)

In Act v Cleopatra presents to Dolabella her vision of Antony in imagery of breath-taking grandeur, looking up and down the Great Chain of Being and all through the cosmos for terms of comparison:

> His face was as the heav'ns, and therein stuck
> A sun and moon, which kept their course and lighted
> The little O, the earth.
> ....
> His legs bestrid the ocean; his rear'd arm
> Crested the world. His voice was propertied
> As all the tuned spheres,. . .
> ....
> .... His delights
> Were dolphin-like.   (V, ii, 82–9)

Who but Shakespeare would dare to puncture such a speech thus:

> CLEOPATRA   Think you there was or might be such a man
>   As this I dreamt of?
> DOLABELLA   Gentle madam, no.

And who else would leave us with the feeling that Cleopatra's vision both is and is not true? The play's vision of the *range* of possibilities within a single human life cuts across the simply ethical dimension – which, of course, is amply represented, too, as in 'the triple pillar of the world transform'd / Into a strumpet's fool'—and no analysis can exhaust the reasons why we are so moved at 'a lass unparallel'd'.

Antony and Cleopatra shows Shakespeare's awareness that human experience is often intangible and ultimately, at its highest reaches or lowest depths, mysterious. It is amorphous and chaotic. 'The web of our life is of a mingled yarn, good and ill together.' We look to our poets to illuminate the mysteries and to our dramatists to make order out of the chaos. It was the achievement of the greatest poet-dramatist to create such order without destroying the mystery of human personality and human fate. His lines were indeed 'so richly spun, and wouen so fit', but, as in Desdemona's handkerchief, there was also magic in the web.

8

SHAKESPEARE'S NARRATIVE POEMS

J. W. LEVER

In all editions of Shakespeare's collected works, his poems appear after the entire body of thirty-seven plays, making up a kind of non-dramatic appendix. Tradition alone explains this position, with its suggestion of second-class matter. Down the centuries editors have respectfully followed the broad lay-out of the First Folio, which included only the dramas; when in 1778 the poems were added, it seemed inevitable that they should be tacked on at the end of the familiar sequence. There they have since remained. Yet as an introduction to Shakespeare's complex genius, the narrative poems at least might have been more suitably placed at the head of his works. In order of composition *Venus and Adonis*, published in 1593, was not likely to have been what Shakespeare in his dedication termed 'the first heir of my invention', but it was certainly his first work to appear in print. *The Rape of Lucrece* followed in the next year, when the only plays yet published were *Titus Andronicus* and the unauthorized quarto of *2 Henry VI*. More important than matters of chronology, these poems give a striking impression of the energy and range of the early Shakespeare; more so, indeed, than his first experiments on the stage. Written at a time when the theatres were closed on account of plague in the capital, they belong to a phase of rapid maturing and awareness of latent powers. Into them was poured a ferment of intuitions, perceptions, speculations and fancies that had not yet found dramatic expression. Many of the sonnets have these qualities and often show close resemblances in attitudes, imagery and turn of phrase; but as a personal medium they stand at a further remove from the plays. The narrative poems were, in the truest sense, the 'first heirs' of Shakespeare's literary creation.

Both *Venus and Adonis* and *Lucrece* were widely read and admired in their time; both, however, can mislead a modern reader who comes to them unprepared. Their unchecked exuberance, ornamentation and profusion of trope and conceit were characteristic of the younger Shakespeare and the age he grew up in: they were not, as they might be in a present-day writer, marks of a superficial talent. Also the poems need to be seen in their respective settings if their tone is to be understood. *Venus and Adonis* has been thought at once too sensuous and too cold, too fleshly and too abstract, too absurd in its situations and yet too tragic in nuance. *Lucrece* has seemed an undramatic drama, too static for the stage, too rhetorical for narrative verse. Such reactions, sincere as they may be, arise from a half-conscious application of standards foreign to the poems themselves. These poems are not 'dramatic', nor are they 'narrative' in the usually accepted sense. They work through their distinctive modes, mythological romance in the case of *Venus and Adonis*, tragical morality in that of *Lucrece*. Through the channels of these Elizabethan forms they aimed at reconciling a variety of effects. Success was not total, but by and large the medium of myth in *Venus and Adonis* brought a wide range of attitudes into accord. Elements of humour and pathos, sensuous and intellectual perceptions combined. With some minor and local flaws, the poem is a triumphant example of diversity in unity. In *Lucrece* the results were less even. The morality form was not so flexible as that of myth, and structurally the poem was unwieldy. There are nevertheless passages of remarkable power, and the first part at least is an outstanding achievement.

Mythological romance gained marked popularity in the last years of the sixteenth century. Introduced by Lodge in *Scilla's Metamorphosis* (1589), it was taken up by Marlowe, Drayton and others. The common inspiration was Ovid's *Metamorphoses*, which offered not only a wealth of story material but also a form that crystallized an acute awareness of the beauty, sensuousness and multiplicity of nature. Ovid's tales presented a virginal world without history or morality. It was inhabited by figures who were creatures of impulse embodying divine or natural forces, archetypes rather than many-sided human beings. Their pursuits, flights, ardours and recoils not so much reflected as prefigured the behaviour of social man. Loveliness and horror, desire and death, were part of their world, but these were regarded with a calm, half-ironic detachment that held the reader's interest, while keeping him at a distance from full imaginative participation. Happenings that in other mediums would evoke pained, erotic or amused responses followed in smooth sequence without arresting the unperturbed narrative flow. In this realm of myth the springs of human experience could be descried and mapped out with a clarity no other medium could provide.

Shakespeare borrowed the outline of *Venus and Adonis* fom Ovid's tale in *Metamorphoses* x, but took details from some of the other stories. Adonis was described by Ovid as a willing young lover with whom Venus enjoyed the pastoral life for an unspecified period, dressing herself as a huntress and joining in the chase against timid hares and deer, though warning him against dangerous beasts. In Shakespeare the events were compressed into a single summer's day and night. At dawn the immortal goddess visited an 'earthly son' and proceeded to woo him with all her charms. Adonis, a coy, self-regarding adolescent, rejected her through the hours of daylight. Aspiring to another kind of manly prowess, he chose that night to hunt the boar, and was killed for his pains. Next morning Venus discovered his body: in her grief she forsook the world and laid a curse on human love, henceforth to be linked with perverseness, cruelty and suffering. As a model of how the spirit of Ovidian narrative might be carried over into English verse, *Scilla's Metamorphosis* set a good formal precedent. Lodge's six-line stanzas had grace and poise; they kept the action moving easily, while allowing scope for elaboration. Early in the poem the story of Adonis was alluded to, with the death of 'the sweet Arcadian boy' and Venus's agonized laments:

> How on his senseless corse she lay a-crying,
> As if the boy were then but new a-dying.

And there were clear hints for the courtship of Adonis in the description of a disdainful Glaucus wooed by the enamoured sea-nymph Scilla:

> How oft with blushes would she plead for grace,
> How oft with whisp'rings would she tempt his ears:
> How oft with crystal did she wet his face:
> How oft she wiped them with her amber hairs:
> So oft, methought I oft in heart desired
> To see the end whereto disdain aspired.

Shakespeare's imagination was engaged on a variety of levels, and the story as he reconceived it had a complexity of its own. Ovid's Arcadian landscape merged insensibly with the English countryside, its downs and woodlands, pastures and hedgerows, foxes and hares, with the noises of hunting dogs and lark-song up on high. There was inherent comedy in the situation of the love-sick goddess of love, frustrated by a callow boy who pouted and turned away his face from her kiss. Setting and situation came together happily in the escapade of Adonis's horse, the paragon of its kind, who breaks his rein and gallops away to answer the call of 'A breeding jennet, lusty, young and proud'; the natural courtship of the animals supplying implicit comment on the waywardness of the young human male. Lovers' follies, and the worse follies of those who rejected love, would be matter for future romantic comedies teaching the lesson 'Make the most of the present time'. In the Arden of *As You Like It* and the woods of *A Midsummer Night's Dream* a range of perverse attitudes would be ex-